## GLENCOE LANGUAGE ARTS

# VOCABULARY POWER

## GRADE 7

**Glencoe McGraw-Hill**

New York, New York    Columbus, Ohio    Woodland Hills, California    Peoria, Illinois

## To the Student

This *Vocabulary Power* workbook gives you the practice you need to expand your vocabulary and improve your ability to understand what you read. Each lesson focuses on a single vocabulary concept or on a theme that ties together the list of words in the Word Bank. You then have several opportunities to learn the words by completing exercises on definitions, context clues, and word parts.

You can keep track of your own progress and achievement in vocabulary study by using the Student Progress Chart, which appears on page v. With your teacher's help, you can score your work on any lesson or test. After you know your score, use the Scoring Scale on pages vi–vii to figure your percentage. Then mark your score (or percentage correct) on the Student Progress Chart. Share your Progress Chart with your parents or guardians as your teacher directs.

## Glencoe/McGraw-Hill

*A Division of The **McGraw-Hill** Companies*

Send all inquiries to:
Glencoe/McGraw-Hill
8787 Orion Place
Columbus, Ohio 43240

ISBN 0-07-826226-7

Printed in the United States of America

21 22 23   HES   13 12 11

# CONTENTS

# STUDENT PROGRESS CHART

Fill in the chart below with your scores, using the scoring scale on the next page.

**Name:** _____

|  | Lesson | Unit Review | Unit Test |
|---|---|---|---|
| 1 | | | |
| 2 | | | |
| 3 | | | |
| 4 | | | |
| 5 | | | |
| Review | | | |
| Test | | | |
| 6 | | | |
| 7 | | | |
| 8 | | | |
| 9 | | | |
| Review | | | |
| Test | | | |
| 10 | | | |
| 11 | | | |
| 12 | | | |
| 13 | | | |
| 14 | | | |
| Review | | | |
| Test | | | |
| 15 | | | |
| 16 | | | |
| 17 | | | |
| 18 | | | |
| Review | | | |
| Test | | | |
| 19 | | | |
| 20 | | | |
| 21 | | | |
| 22 | | | |
| Review | | | |
| Test | | | |
| 23 | | | |
| 24 | | | |
| 25 | | | |
| 26 | | | |
| 27 | | | |
| 28 | | | |
| Review | | | |
| Test | | | |
| 29 | | | |
| 30 | | | |
| 31 | | | |
| 32 | | | |
| Review | | | |
| Test | | | |
| 33 | | | |
| 34 | | | |
| 35 | | | |
| 36 | | | |
| Review | | | |
| Test | | | |

# SCORING SCALE

Use this scale to find your score. Line up the number of items with the number correct. For example, if 15 out of 16 items are correct, the score is 93.7 percent (see grayed area).

## Number Correct

| Number of Items | 1 | 2 | 3 | 4 | 5 | 6 | 7 | 8 | 9 | 10 | 11 | 12 | 13 | 14 | 15 | 16 | 17 | 18 | 19 | 20 |
|---|---|---|---|---|---|---|---|---|---|---|---|---|---|---|---|---|---|---|---|---|
| 1 | 100 | | | | | | | | | | | | | | | | | | | |
| 2 | 50 | 100 | | | | | | | | | | | | | | | | | | |
| 3 | 33.3 | 66.7 | 100 | | | | | | | | | | | | | | | | | |
| 4 | 25 | 50 | 75 | 100 | | | | | | | | | | | | | | | | |
| 5 | 20 | 40 | 60 | 80 | 100 | | | | | | | | | | | | | | | |
| 6 | 16.7 | 33.3 | 50 | 66.7 | 83.3 | 100 | | | | | | | | | | | | | | |
| 7 | 14.3 | 28.6 | 42.9 | 57.1 | 71.4 | 85.7 | 100 | | | | | | | | | | | | | |
| 8 | 12.5 | 25 | 37.5 | 50 | 62.5 | 75 | 87.5 | 100 | | | | | | | | | | | | |
| 9 | 11.1 | 22.2 | 33.3 | 44.4 | 55.6 | 66.7 | 77.8 | 88.9 | 100 | | | | | | | | | | | |
| 10 | 10 | 20 | 30 | 40 | 50 | 60 | 70 | 80 | 90 | 100 | | | | | | | | | | |
| 11 | 9.1 | 18.1 | 27.2 | 36.3 | 45.4 | 54.5 | 63.6 | 72.7 | 81.8 | 90.9 | 100 | | | | | | | | | |
| 12 | 8.3 | 16.7 | 25 | 33.3 | 41.7 | 50 | 58.3 | 66.7 | 75 | 83.3 | 91.7 | 100 | | | | | | | | |
| 13 | 7.7 | 15.3 | 23.1 | 30.8 | 38.5 | 46.1 | 53.8 | 61.5 | 69.2 | 76.9 | 84.6 | 92.3 | 100 | | | | | | | |
| 14 | 7.1 | 14.3 | 21.4 | 28.6 | 35.7 | 42.8 | 50 | 57.1 | 64.3 | 71.4 | 78.5 | 85.7 | 92.8 | 100 | | | | | | |
| 15 | 6.7 | 13.3 | 20 | 26.7 | 33.3 | 40 | 46.6 | 53.3 | 60 | 66.7 | 73.3 | 80 | 86.7 | 93.3 | 100 | | | | | |
| 16 | 6.3 | 12.5 | 18.8 | 25 | 31.2 | 37.5 | 43.7 | 50 | 56.2 | 62.5 | 68.7 | 75 | 81.2 | 87.5 | 93.7 | 100 | | | | |
| 17 | 5.9 | 11.8 | 17.6 | 23.5 | 29.4 | 35.3 | 41.2 | 47 | 52.9 | 58.8 | 64.7 | 70.6 | 76.5 | 82.3 | 88.2 | 94.1 | 100 | | | |
| 18 | 5.6 | 11.1 | 16.7 | 22.2 | 27.8 | 33.3 | 38.9 | 44.4 | 50 | 55.5 | 61.1 | 66.7 | 72.2 | 77.8 | 83.3 | 88.9 | 94.4 | 100 | | |
| 19 | 5.3 | 10.5 | 15.8 | 21 | 26.3 | 31.6 | 36.8 | 42.1 | 47.4 | 52.6 | 57.9 | 63.1 | 68.4 | 73.7 | 78.9 | 84.2 | 89.4 | 94.7 | 100 | |
| 20 | 5 | 10 | 15 | 20 | 25 | 30 | 35 | 40 | 45 | 50 | 55 | 60 | 65 | 70 | 75 | 80 | 85 | 90 | 95 | 100 |
| 21 | 4.8 | 9.5 | 14.3 | 19 | 23.8 | 28.6 | 33.3 | 38.1 | 42.8 | 47.6 | 52.3 | 57.1 | 61.9 | 66.7 | 71.4 | 76.1 | 80.9 | 85.7 | 90.5 | 95.2 |
| 22 | 4.5 | 9.1 | 13.7 | 18.2 | 22.7 | 27.3 | 31.8 | 36.4 | 40.9 | 45.4 | 50 | 54.5 | 59.1 | 63.6 | 68.1 | 72.7 | 77.2 | 81.8 | 86.4 | 90.9 |
| 23 | 4.3 | 8.7 | 13 | 17.4 | 21.7 | 26.1 | 30.4 | 34.8 | 39.1 | 43.5 | 47.8 | 52.1 | 56.5 | 60.8 | 65.2 | 69.5 | 73.9 | 78.3 | 82.6 | 86.9 |
| 24 | 4.2 | 8.3 | 12.5 | 16.7 | 20.8 | 25 | 29.2 | 33.3 | 37.5 | 41.7 | 45.8 | 50 | 54.2 | 58.3 | 62.5 | 66.7 | 70.8 | 75 | 79.1 | 83.3 |
| 25 | 4 | 8 | 12 | 16 | 20 | 24 | 28 | 32 | 36 | 40 | 44 | 48 | 52 | 56 | 60 | 64 | 68 | 72 | 76 | 80 |
| 26 | 3.8 | 7.7 | 11.5 | 15.4 | 19.2 | 23.1 | 26.9 | 30.8 | 34.6 | 38.5 | 42.3 | 46.2 | 50 | 53.8 | 57.7 | 61.5 | 65.4 | 69.2 | 73.1 | 76.9 |
| 27 | 3.7 | 7.4 | 11.1 | 14.8 | 18.5 | 22.2 | 25.9 | 29.6 | 33.3 | 37 | 40.7 | 44.4 | 48.1 | 51.9 | 55.6 | 59.2 | 63 | 66.7 | 70.4 | 74.1 |
| 28 | 3.6 | 7.1 | 10.7 | 14.3 | 17.9 | 21.4 | 25 | 28.6 | 32.1 | 35.7 | 39.3 | 42.9 | 46.4 | 50 | 53.6 | 57.1 | 60.7 | 64.3 | 67.9 | 71.4 |
| 29 | 3.4 | 6.9 | 10.3 | 13.8 | 17.2 | 20.7 | 24.1 | 27.6 | 31 | 34.5 | 37.9 | 41.4 | 44.8 | 48.3 | 51.7 | 55.2 | 58.6 | 62.1 | 65.5 | 69 |
| 30 | 3.3 | 6.7 | 10 | 13.3 | 16.7 | 20 | 23.3 | 26.7 | 30 | 33.3 | 36.7 | 40 | 43.3 | 46.7 | 50 | 53.3 | 56.7 | 60 | 63.3 | 66.7 |
| 31 | 3.2 | 6.5 | 9.7 | 13 | 16.1 | 19.3 | 22.6 | 25.8 | 29 | 32.2 | 35.4 | 38.7 | 41.9 | 45.1 | 48.3 | 51.6 | 54.8 | 58 | 61.2 | 64.5 |
| 32 | 3.1 | 6.3 | 9.4 | 12.5 | 15.6 | 18.8 | 21.9 | 25 | 28.1 | 31.3 | 34.4 | 37.5 | 40.6 | 43.8 | 46.9 | 50 | 53.1 | 56.2 | 59.4 | 62.5 |
| 33 | 3 | 6 | 9 | 12.1 | 15.1 | 18.1 | 21.2 | 24.2 | 27.2 | 30.3 | 33 | 36.3 | 39.3 | 42.4 | 45.4 | 48.4 | 51.5 | 54.5 | 57.5 | 60.6 |
| 34 | 2.9 | 5.9 | 8.8 | 11.8 | 14.7 | 17.6 | 20.6 | 23.5 | 26.5 | 29.4 | 32.4 | 35.3 | 38.2 | 41.2 | 44.1 | 47.1 | 50 | 52.9 | 55.9 | 58.8 |
| 35 | 2.9 | 5.7 | 8.6 | 11.4 | 14.3 | 17.1 | 20 | 22.9 | 25.7 | 28.6 | 31.4 | 34.3 | 37.1 | 40 | 42.9 | 45.7 | 48.6 | 51.4 | 54.3 | 57.1 |
| 36 | 2.8 | 5.6 | 8.3 | 11.1 | 13.9 | 16.7 | 19.4 | 22.2 | 25 | 27.8 | 30.6 | 33.3 | 36.1 | 38.9 | 41.7 | 44.4 | 47.2 | 50 | 52.7 | 55.6 |
| 37 | 2.7 | 5.4 | 8.1 | 10.8 | 13.5 | 16.2 | 18.9 | 21.6 | 24.3 | 27 | 29.7 | 32.4 | 35.1 | 37.8 | 40.5 | 43.2 | 45.9 | 48.6 | 51.4 | 54 |
| 38 | 2.6 | 5.3 | 7.9 | 10.5 | 13.2 | 15.8 | 18.4 | 21.1 | 23.7 | 26.3 | 28.9 | 31.6 | 34.2 | 36.8 | 39.5 | 42.1 | 44.7 | 47.4 | 50 | 52.6 |
| 39 | 2.6 | 5.2 | 7.7 | 10.3 | 12.8 | 15.4 | 17.9 | 20.5 | 23.1 | 25.6 | 28.2 | 30.8 | 33.3 | 35.9 | 38.5 | 41 | 43.6 | 46.2 | 48.7 | 51.3 |
| 40 | 2.5 | 5 | 7.5 | 10 | 12.5 | 15 | 17.5 | 20 | 22.5 | 25 | 27.5 | 30 | 32.5 | 35 | 37.5 | 40 | 42.5 | 45 | 47.5 | 50 |

## Number Correct

| Number of Items | 21 | 22 | 23 | 24 | 25 | 26 | 27 | 28 | 29 | 30 | 31 | 32 | 33 | 34 | 35 | 36 | 37 | 38 | 39 | 40 |
|---|---|---|---|---|---|---|---|---|---|---|---|---|---|---|---|---|---|---|---|---|
| 1 | | | | | | | | | | | | | | | | | | | | |
| 2 | | | | | | | | | | | | | | | | | | | | |
| 3 | | | | | | | | | | | | | | | | | | | | |
| 4 | | | | | | | | | | | | | | | | | | | | |
| 5 | | | | | | | | | | | | | | | | | | | | |
| 6 | | | | | | | | | | | | | | | | | | | | |
| 7 | | | | | | | | | | | | | | | | | | | | |
| 8 | | | | | | | | | | | | | | | | | | | | |
| 9 | | | | | | | | | | | | | | | | | | | | |
| 10 | | | | | | | | | | | | | | | | | | | | |
| 11 | | | | | | | | | | | | | | | | | | | | |
| 12 | | | | | | | | | | | | | | | | | | | | |
| 13 | | | | | | | | | | | | | | | | | | | | |
| 14 | | | | | | | | | | | | | | | | | | | | |
| 15 | | | | | | | | | | | | | | | | | | | | |
| 16 | | | | | | | | | | | | | | | | | | | | |
| 17 | | | | | | | | | | | | | | | | | | | | |
| 18 | | | | | | | | | | | | | | | | | | | | |
| 19 | | | | | | | | | | | | | | | | | | | | |
| 20 | | | | | | | | | | | | | | | | | | | | |
| 21 | 100 | | | | | | | | | | | | | | | | | | | |
| 22 | 95.4 | 100 | | | | | | | | | | | | | | | | | | |
| 23 | 91.3 | 95.6 | 100 | | | | | | | | | | | | | | | | | |
| 24 | 87.5 | 91.6 | 95.8 | 100 | | | | | | | | | | | | | | | | |
| 25 | 84 | 88 | 92 | 96 | 100 | | | | | | | | | | | | | | | |
| 26 | 80.8 | 84.6 | 88.5 | 92.3 | 96.2 | 100 | | | | | | | | | | | | | | |
| 27 | 77.8 | 81.5 | 85.2 | 88.9 | 92.6 | 96.3 | 100 | | | | | | | | | | | | | |
| 28 | 75 | 78.6 | 82.1 | 85.7 | 89.3 | 92.9 | 96.4 | 100 | | | | | | | | | | | | |
| 29 | 72.4 | 75.9 | 79.3 | 82.8 | 86.2 | 89.7 | 93.1 | 96.6 | 100 | | | | | | | | | | | |
| 30 | 70 | 73.3 | 76.7 | 80 | 83.3 | 86.7 | 90 | 93.3 | 96.7 | 100 | | | | | | | | | | |
| 31 | 67.7 | 70.9 | 74.2 | 77.4 | 80.6 | 83.9 | 87.1 | 90.3 | 93.5 | 96.8 | 100 | | | | | | | | | |
| 32 | 65.6 | 68.8 | 71.9 | 75 | 78.1 | 81.2 | 84.4 | 87.5 | 90.6 | 93.8 | 96.9 | 100 | | | | | | | | |
| 33 | 63.6 | 66.7 | 69.7 | 72.7 | 75.8 | 78.8 | 81.8 | 84.8 | 87.8 | 90.9 | 93.9 | 96.9 | 100 | | | | | | | |
| 34 | 61.8 | 64.7 | 67.6 | 70.6 | 73.5 | 76.5 | 79.4 | 82.4 | 85.3 | 88.2 | 91.2 | 94.1 | 97.1 | 100 | | | | | | |
| 35 | 60 | 62.9 | 65.7 | 68.6 | 71.4 | 74.3 | 77.1 | 80 | 82.9 | 85.7 | 88.6 | 91.4 | 94.3 | 97.1 | 100 | | | | | |
| 36 | 58.3 | 61.1 | 63.8 | 66.7 | 69.4 | 72.2 | 75 | 77.8 | 80.6 | 83.3 | 86.1 | 88.9 | 91.7 | 94.4 | 97.2 | 100 | | | | |
| 37 | 56.8 | 59.5 | 62.2 | 64.9 | 67.6 | 70.3 | 72.9 | 75.7 | 78.4 | 81.1 | 83.8 | 86.5 | 89.2 | 91.9 | 94.6 | 97.3 | 100 | | | |
| 38 | 55.3 | 57.9 | 60.5 | 63.2 | 65.8 | 68.4 | 71.1 | 73.7 | 76.3 | 78.9 | 81.6 | 84.2 | 86.8 | 89.5 | 92.1 | 94.7 | 97.3 | 100 | | |
| 39 | 53.8 | 56.4 | 58.9 | 61.5 | 64.1 | 66.7 | 69.2 | 71.8 | 74.4 | 76.9 | 79.5 | 82.1 | 84.6 | 87.2 | 89.7 | 92.3 | 94.9 | 97.4 | 100 | |
| 40 | 52.5 | 55 | 57.5 | 60 | 62.5 | 65 | 67.5 | 70 | 72.5 | 75 | 77.5 | 80 | 82.5 | 85 | 87.5 | 90 | 92.5 | 95 | 97.5 | 100 |

# Vocabulary Power

## Lesson 1  Using Synonyms

Have you ever thought about what makes you who you are? People are a combination of many different things. The influence of your parents and families plays a big part. So does what you learn in school and from friends. Beliefs and values are also important. Even your biological make-up has a major role. The words in this lesson can help you explore the different elements that make you who you are.

### Word List

| | | | |
|---|---|---|---|
| agile | manufacture | rashly | trivial |
| divulge | naive | specify | wholeheartedly |
| erratic | propel | | |

### EXERCISE A  Synonyms

**Synonyms are words with similar meanings. Each boldfaced vocabulary word below is paired with a synonym whose meaning you probably know. Think of other words related to the synonym and write them on the line provided. Then, look up the word in a dictionary and write its meaning.**

1. **manufacture** : make _____

   Dictionary definition _____

2. **wholeheartedly** : sincerely _____

   Dictionary definition _____

3. **divulge** : reveal _____

   Dictionary definition _____

4. **rashly** : recklessly _____

   Dictionary definition _____

5. **propel** : push _____

   Dictionary definition _____

6. **erratic** : inconsistent _____

   Dictionary definition _____

7. **specify** : state _____

   Dictionary definition _____

## Vocabulary Power *continued*

8. **agile** : quick _____

Dictionary definition _____

9. **naive** : unsophisticated _____

Dictionary definition _____

10. **trivial** : unimportant _____

Dictionary definition _____

**EXERCISE B** **Sentence Completion**

**Write the vocabulary word that best completes the sentence.**

1. Hayley acted _____ by volunteering for the unspecified task.

2. The spider monkeys at the zoo were unbelievably _____, swinging from branch

   to branch.

3. Please don't treat my questions as if they are _____—they're important to me!

4. The workers received bribes to _____ information about the top-secret project.

5. The new plant on the edge of town will _____ seat belts for cars.

6. I cheered _____ when our neighbor was on the television game show.

7. If you don't _____ which CD you want, you might receive the wrong one.

8. It's amazing how fast the wind can _____ the sailboat over the lake.

9. While their path seemed _____, the ants knew exactly where they were going.

10. How could you be _____ enough to believe that you could buy a computer for $29?

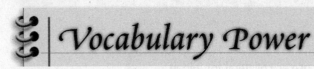

# Vocabulary Power

## Lesson 2  Multiple-Meaning Words

If you're like most people your age, you probably need more time and input to make decisions about your future. Even if your dreams change and take different shapes, it's important to keep telling yourself that you can achieve your personal goals if you're willing to work for them. In this lesson, you'll learn words related to personal dreams and goals.

**Word List**

| | | | |
|---|---|---|---|
| apathy | comply | exotic | neglected |
| asset | emerge | motive | resigned |
| burden | exhibit | | |

### EXERCISE A  Multiple-Meaning Words

**Use context clues to determine the meaning of the boldfaced word. Then, write the dictionary definition that applies.**

1. Not wanting to **burden** her mother further, Sally rode her bike to soccer practice.

_____

2. Greg was **resigned** to helping his father build a shed all weekend.

_____

3. **Exhibit** A at the trial was a tearstained letter of farewell from the dying wife.

_____

4. Lou felt only **apathy** toward the student proposal about fees.

_____

5. Phil the Groundhog had to **emerge** from his hole before the witnesses could declare an early spring.

_____

6. We studied **motive** energy in physics class last month.

_____

7. Courtiers had to **comply** with court protocol when they had an audience with King George.

_____

## 🎼 *Vocabulary Power* *continued*

8. The loan officer told me that I need to have an **asset** to use as collateral for a loan.

   _____

9. James was reprimanded because he **neglected** to salute his superior officer.

   _____

10. The giant panda at our zoo is **exotic**—it's native to China!

   _____

### EXERCISE B  Questions and Answers
**Answer each question based on your understanding of the boldfaced word.**

1. What do you feel is the best way to get people to **comply** with antilittering laws?

   _____

2. What actions might you take if you are feeling **neglected** by your friends?

   _____

3. What do you feel is your strongest **asset** as a member of a class committee?

   _____

4. Describe an **exotic** place you would like to visit and explain why you would like to visit it.

   _____

5. Is student **apathy** a problem at your school? Why or why not?

   _____

6. Describe the mood of the movie audience at the moment when the monster is about to **emerge**

   from the darkness. _____

7. Describe a time when you felt **resigned** to a situation.

   _____

8. What might be someone's **motive** for doing volunteer work?

   _____

# Vocabulary Power

## Lesson 3  Word Parts

Words can be made up of different parts. The main meaning of a word is contained in its root or base word. Base words are roots that are complete words. Prefixes can be added to the beginning of a root and suffixes at the end to change the word's meaning. Knowing the meanings of word roots, prefixes, and suffixes can help you make an educated guess about the meaning of a new word. Sometimes, however, the exact meaning of the new word isn't clear from the root. It's always safer to look up new words in a dictionary. In this lesson, you'll identify some common roots, prefixes, and suffixes and learn how they work together to give meaning to words.

**Word List**

| | | | |
|---|---|---|---|
| auditorium | dissension | provide | sensitize |
| auditory | dissent | providence | visible |
| consent | inaudible | | |

**EXERCISE A**  Context Clues
**Read the clues and answer each question.**

1. *Vis, vid* is a Latin root meaning "to see." If the prefix *pro-,* meaning "before" or "forward," is added to this root, what might be the meaning of the word **provide?** _____

   _____

2. Adding the suffix *-ence,* which makes words into nouns, creates **providence,** a word that means what?

   _____

3. The suffix *-ible* is used to create adjectives from roots. How would you describe something that is **visible?** _____

4. The Latin root *aud, audi* means "to hear." The suffix *-tory* is used to make adjectives. Which part of your body contains its **auditory** sense? _____

5. The Latin suffix *-ium* describes rooms or buildings. What kinds of activities go on in an **auditorium?** _____

6. The prefix *in-* is one of many that means "not" or "the opposite of." What are some things that you might describe as **inaudible?** _____

7. A Latin root meaning "to feel" is *sens/sent.* *Con-* is a prefix that means "with." If you **consent** to something, what might you be doing? _____

## Vocabulary Power *continued*

8. The prefix *dis-* is another "not" prefix. If you **dissent,** how do you feel about a suggestion?

_____

9. Adding the noun suffix *-ion* to *dissent* creates the noun **dissension,** which probably means what?

_____

10. A suffix that is used to create verbs is *-ize*. If you **sensitize** others to your situation, how would

they feel? _____

### EXERCISE B  Defining Words
**Check your definitions by looking up each word in a dictionary. Write the meaning. How close did you come to the correct meaning?**

1. provide _____

2. providence _____

3. visible _____

4. auditory _____

5. auditorium _____

6. inaudible _____

7. consent _____

8. dissent _____

9. dissension _____

10. sensitize _____

### EXERCISE C  Word Webs
**On another sheet of paper, make three copies of the word web on this page. Using word parts you learned about in this lesson, write a word root in the first web, a prefix in the second web, and a suffix in the third web. Then, fill in the "rays" with as many words as you can that contain that root, prefix, or suffix. Exchange webs with a partner and discuss the meanings of the words you have listed.**

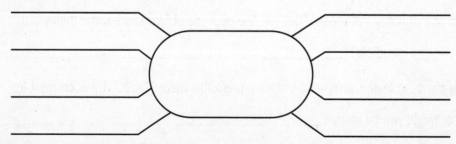

# Vocabulary Power

## Lesson 4  Word Families

Word families are groups of words that contain the same roots or base words. The root or base word gives a word its main meaning. In this lesson, you'll learn about words in the same word families.

**Word List**

| | | | |
|---|---|---|---|
| deport | diction | patriotic | prescribe |
| dictate | inscription | portable | scribble |
| dictator | paternal | | |

**EXERCISE A**  Dictionary Definitions

**Look up each word in a dictionary and write its meaning. Use the information in the dictionary entry to underline the root or base word.**

1. portable _____

2. deport _____

3. paternal _____

4. patriotic _____

5. scribble _____

6. inscription _____

7. prescribe _____

8. dictate _____

9. diction _____

10. dictator _____

**EXERCISE B**  Sentence Completion

**Write the vocabulary word that best completes the sentence.**

1. If you _____ your speech, I will type it for you.

2. When the storm knocked out our power last summer, we had to borrow my uncle's

   _____ electric generator.

3. The football player decided to _____ his autograph quickly on the napkin.

4. Tabitha's _____ grandmother was an underwater explorer and scientist.

# Vocabulary Power *continued*

5. The doctor decided to _____ a painkiller for Marcie's sprained ankle.

6. The speaker was quite easy to understand because his _____ was perfect.

7. According to my grandfather, it is every person's _____ duty to join the armed forces and fight for the nation.

8. People marched in the streets in protest when the president seized complete control of the country and became a _____.

9. The _____ on the ancient tombstone was worn and hard to read.

10. The judge was forced to _____ the foreign workers since they were in the country illegally.

## EXERCISE C  Usage
**Answer each question based on your understanding of the boldfaced word.**

1. Who can **prescribe** drugs for you if you are sick?

   _____

2. Which item is most easily **portable**—a watch, a canoe, or a pony?

   _____

3. Why is it important to pay attention to your **diction** when you are giving a speech?

   _____

4. What **inscription** might you add to the base of a statue of your hero?

   _____

5. Do you think it's important to feel **patriotic**? Why or why not?

   _____

*Vocabulary Power*

## Lesson 5  Using Reference Skills
### Using a Dictionary Entry
You already know that a dictionary is a valuable source of definitions. The words defined in a dictionary are called entries. Look at the sample entry below.

**Guidewords**

independent/indicator

**Pronunciation spelling**

**Entry**

**indicate** (in′ də kāt′) *v.* **1.** to point out or point to: *I will indicate when we should leave.* **2.** to be a sign of: *The red spots on his skin indicate measles.* **3.** to demonstrate the necessity of: *The crowded conditions indicate the need for a new school building.* **4.** suggest, state briefly: *I indicate agreement by nodding my head.*

**Definition(s)**      **Sample phrase or sentence**

**EXERCISE**

**Use the sample entry to answer each question.**

1. Which entry would you find on this page, *indefinite, index,* or *individual?* _____

2. Which meaning of *indicate* is being used in the following sentence?

   The darkening clouds *indicated* the storm's approach. _____

3. On which syllable does the major accent fall in the word *indicate?* _____

4. Use the third meaning of *indicate* in a sentence of your own.

   _____

5. Use the fourth meaning of *indicate* in a sentence of your own.

   _____

6. What guidewords might be on the pages before and after the page of this entry?

   before  _____

   after  _____

7. Use the second meaning of *indicate* in a sentence of your own.

   _____

# *Vocabulary Power*

## Review: Unit 1

**EXERCISE**

**Circle the word in parentheses that best completes each sentence.**

1. We started a poster campaign to get students involved in school issues and to fight (apathy, burden, providence).

2. As the sun rose, the dark outline of the mountain peak slowly became (patriotic, erratic, visible).

3. It's best not to get upset about (paternal, inaudible, trivial) or unimportant matters.

4. The brightly colored birds are from (naive, portable, exotic) locations around the world.

5. The explorer read the strange (inscription, asset, motive) on the ancient treasure chest with growing excitement.

6. Paul promised not to (divulge, consent, prescribe) the secret I whispered to him.

7. Because he was almost fifteen years older than his younger brother, Mark's feelings for Michael were more (naive, paternal, trivial) than brotherly.

8. The crowded conditions and harsh rules in the prison caused feelings of (dictator, diction, dissension) among the prisoners.

9. You have to be (exotic, agile, patriotic) to complete the obstacle course.

10. We must find a way to make drivers (comply, dissent, propel) with the speed limit.

# Vocabulary Power

## Test: Unit 1

**PART A**

**Circle the letter of the word that best completes the sentence.**

1. The police wondered about the man's _____ for committing the crime.
   **a.** apathy      **b.** motive      **c.** providence      **d.** diction

2. You'll have to improve your _____ if you want people to understand what you are saying.
   **a.** diction      **b.** burden      **c.** asset      **d.** exhibit

3. Only a _____ person would tell a stranger his credit card number.
   **a.** paternal      **b.** naive      **c.** portable      **d.** visible

4. The pilgrims gave thanks to _____ for their plentiful harvest.
   **a.** his dictator      **b.** the inscription      **c.** providence      **d.** the burden

5. The photographers waited for the groundhog to _____ from his hole.
   **a.** deport      **b.** propel      **c.** provide      **d.** emerge

6. I hope the doctor can _____ something strong for this toothache!
   **a.** prescribe      **b.** divulge      **c.** exhibit      **d.** dissent

7. Because she couldn't change the judge's decision, Shelley became _____ to it.
   **a.** divulged      **b.** prescribed      **c.** resigned      **d.** neglected

8. I'll write down the message if you _____ it slowly and clearly for me.
   **a.** propel      **b.** dictate      **c.** comply      **d.** exhibit

9. Have you decided which seashells to _____ in the showcase?
   **a.** consent      **b.** divulge      **c.** deport      **d.** exhibit

10. The company president explained that the new factory would _____ compact discs.
    **a.** dictate      **b.** exhibit      **c.** propel      **d.** manufacture

11. I could see the stage all right, but the _____ quality was poor.
    **a.** exotic      **b.** auditory      **c.** paternal      **d.** agile

12. Taking class notes for you while your broken arm heals won't be a _____ at all.
    **a.** burden      **b.** diction      **c.** dissension      **d.** providence

13. While most club members agreed with the decision, I expect Ricky to _____ forcibly.
    **a.** consent      **b.** comply      **c.** dissent      **d.** scribble

## *Vocabulary Power* *continued*

14. The congresswoman pounded the table and stated that she would never _____ to raising taxes for the poorest taxpayers.
    **a.** consent      **b.** dissent         **c.** dictate        **d.** prescribe

15. Will made all the decisions for the chess club like a(n) _____, without asking anyone else's opinion.
    **a.** burden       **b.** dictator        **c.** asset          **d.** exhibit

16. If you carelessly _____ the instructions, there's a good chance someone will misunderstand them.
    **a.** propel       **b.** manufacture     **c.** scribble       **d.** deport

17. Think about your answer for a while instead of answering _____.
    **a.** with a scribble   **b.** wholeheartedly   **c.** with a motive   **d.** rashly

18. Because the criminal was a citizen of another country, the judge decided to _____ him instead of sentencing him to jail.
    **a.** divulge      **b.** deport          **c.** specify        **d.** prescribe

19. Doing volunteer work at the animal shelter will certainly _____ you to the problem of too many stray dogs and cats.
    **a.** exhibit      **b.** dictate         **c.** sensitize      **d.** divulge

20. Be sure to _____ that you want the peaches with the red centers.
    **a.** specify      **b.** exhibit         **c.** dictate        **d.** deport

### PART B

**Circle the letter of the expression that best answers the question.**

1. What propels a sailboat through the water?
    **a.** the water        **b.** the captain      **c.** the rudder      **d.** the wind

2. Toward what would a person have patriotic feelings?
    **a.** a baseball team  **b.** a country        **c.** a pet           **d.** a beverage

3. What activity would *not* take place in an auditorium?
    **a.** a rehearsal      **b.** a concert        **c.** a play          **d.** a swimming meet

4. If you are in agreement with a proposal, you would express your _____.
    **a.** asset            **b.** dissent          **c.** consent         **d.** inscription

5. How would you describe having a reputation as an honest person?
    **a.** an asset         **b.** a burden         **c.** a motive        **d.** an exhibit

# Vocabulary Power

## Lesson 6  Using Synonyms

Change is always at work. Some changes are easy to identify, like changes in the weather or the seasons. Other changes are harder to recognize, like the changes in the way you experience the world around you. This lesson presents some words that can be useful in talking about change.

### Word List

| | | | |
|---|---|---|---|
| align | dignity | preview | status |
| bewildered | obsessed | speculation | vary |
| conviction | passive | | |

### EXERCISE A  Synonyms

**Each boldfaced word below is paired with a synonym whose meaning you probably know. Think of other words related to the synonym and write your ideas on the line provided. Then, look up the word in a dictionary and write its definition.**

1. **bewildered** : confused _____

   Dictionary definition _____

2. **speculation** : thinking about something _____

   Dictionary definition _____

3. **conviction** : belief _____

   Dictionary definition _____

4. **obsessed** : overly concerned _____

   Dictionary definition _____

5. **vary** : change _____

   Dictionary definition _____

6. **dignity** : honor _____

   Dictionary definition _____

7. **passive** : inactive _____

   Dictionary definition _____

# Vocabulary Power *continued*

8. **status** : position _____

   Dictionary definition _____

9. **preview** : see beforehand _____

   Dictionary definition _____

10. **align** : bring into line _____

    Dictionary definition _____

## EXERCISE B  Sentence Completion

**Write the vocabulary word that best completes the sentence.**

1. Mr. Pickens lost all his _____ when the clown hit him in the face with a cream pie.

2. The candidate repeated her strong _____ against raising taxes.

3. To open the lock, you have to _____ the two pins with the key.

4. The largest wolf also has the highest _____ in the wolf pack.

5. To bake muffins, the cook must not allow the oven temperature to _____ by more than a few degrees.

6. The newspaper contained much _____ about the outcome of the big game.

7. Film critics got to _____ the movie before it was released for the public.

8. Alicia would get better grades if she weren't so _____ during class.

9. Shawn is so _____ with his computer that he has time for nothing else.

10. I was completely _____ by the complicated instructions.

# Vocabulary Power

## Lesson 7  Using Synonyms

Changes for the better, such as those that result in more happiness or a better life, are always welcome. Other changes, though, like ones that take friends away or in any other way make life less enjoyable, are not. Dealing with both kinds of changes is an important life skill. The words in this lesson relate to how people face changes.

**Word List**

| | | | |
|---|---|---|---|
| assert | drab | perplexity | versatile |
| bias | hardy | sanctuary | wily |
| comprehend | opportunity | | |

### EXERCISE A  Synonyms

**Each boldfaced word below is paired with a synonym whose meaning you probably know. Think of other words related to the synonym and write your ideas on the line provided. Then, look up the word in a dictionary and write its definition.**

1. **opportunity** : a good chance _____

   Dictionary definition _____

2. **perplexity** : confusion _____

   Dictionary definition _____

3. **drab** : dull _____

   Dictionary definition _____

4. **comprehend** : understand _____

   Dictionary definition _____

5. **versatile** : changing _____

   Dictionary definition _____

6. **hardy** : tough _____

   Dictionary definition _____

7. **assert** : declare _____

   Dictionary definition _____

8. **sanctuary** : safe place _____

   Dictionary definition _____

9. **bias** : prejudice _____

   Dictionary definition _____

10. **wily** : clever _____

    Dictionary definition _____

## EXERCISE B  Multiple-Meaning Words

**Many words in English have more than one meaning. Each meaning, however, is based on the meaning of the word root. The word *bias,* for example, comes from the Greek *epikarsios* ("slanted") via the Middle French *biais,* meaning "a slope or slant," to the present form. A dictionary entry for *bias* lists many different meanings, but all of them are related to the root meaning "slanted." Write the part of speech, number, and letter of the definition that fits each sentence.**

---

**bias** *n.* **1.** a line diagonal to the grain of a fabric, *esp.* a line at a 45-degree angle to the selvage **2. a.** a peculiarity in the shape of a bowl or ball that causes it to swerve; **b.** the swerve of the bowl or ball **3. a.** bent, tendency; **b.** an inclination of temperament or outlook, *esp.* a personal and sometimes unreasoned judgment: prejudice; **c.** an instance of such prejudice; **d.** a systematic error introduced into the sampling or testing by selecting or encouraging one outcome or answer over others **4.** voltage applied to a device to establish a reference level for operation *v.* **1.** to give a prejudiced outlook **2.** in radio, to apply a slight negative or positive voltage to an electrode **biased** *adj.* prejudiced **on the bias** *adv.* cut diagonally

---

_____ 1. Teachers complained that the test's language showed **bias** against nonnative speakers.

_____ 2. Questionnaires should be free from **bias** toward a particular outcome.

_____ 3. To achieve the desired effect, the seamstress cut the fabric on the **bias.**

_____ 4. His ownership of the casino **bias(ed)** his voting on the gambling issue.

_____ 5. The radio engineer applied a slight negative **bias** to the electrode.

_____ 6. The bowler calculated the **bias** as he rolled the ball down the lane.

_____ 7. The designer startled the fashion world with garments cut on the **bias.**

_____ 8. His **biased** judgment on the issue of downtown renovation cost him the election.

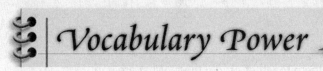

# Vocabulary Power

## Lesson 8  Prefixes That Mean "not" or "the opposite of"

Knowing the meanings of prefixes can help you uncover the meanings of unknown words. A large number of prefixes mean "not" or "the opposite of." Some of these prefixes are *non-, ir-, un-, mal-, anti-, de-, dis-, in-, op-,* and *il-.* Be careful, though. Not all words that begin with these letter combinations have the meaning of the prefix. When in doubt, look up the word in a dictionary.

| **Word List** | | | |
|---|---|---|---|
| antidote | illegible | malfunction | oppose |
| detach | incompetent | noncommittal | unabridged |
| disoriented | irrational | | |

### EXERCISE A  Prefixes

**Underline the prefix in each of the ten boldfaced words. Using the clues, answer the question. Then, check the definition of the vocabulary word in a dictionary and write its meaning.**

1. **noncommittal:** The Latin root *committere* means "to connect, entrust." If you give a

   **noncommittal** answer to a question, how are you replying?

   _____

   Dictionary definition _____

2. **irrational:** The Latin root *ratio* means "reason." What words might you choose to describe a

   person or an action that is **irrational?** _____

   Dictionary definition _____

3. **unabridged:** An abridged dictionary omits some words in a language to save space. What might

   an **unabridged** dictionary contain? _____

   Dictionary definition _____

4. **malfunction:** When a machine functions, it is working properly or according to design. What is

   happening when a machine starts to **malfunction?** _____

   Dictionary definition _____

5. **antidote:** The root of this word comes from the Greek word meaning "to give." If someone

   receives an **antidote** after swallowing poison, what might the effects of such an antidote be?

   _____

   Dictionary definition _____

# Vocabulary Power *continued*

6. **detach:** To attach one thing to another means to put them together or join them. What are you

doing when you **detach** one thing from another? _____

_____

Dictionary definition _____

7. **disoriented:** To orient yourself means to find your location in relation to another point, to get your

bearings, or to find your balance. If you are **disoriented**, how are you feeling?

_____

Dictionary definition _____

8. **incompetent:** Competent workers do their jobs well because they are qualified, knowledgeable,

and well trained. How might **incompetent** workers perform their jobs?

_____

Dictionary definition _____

9. **oppose:** To propose something is to suggest or support it. If you add the negative prefix *ob-* to

the Latin root *ponere* "to put or place," what is the meaning of **oppose?**

_____

Dictionary definition _____

10. **illegible:** The root *leg* comes from a Latin word that means "to read." The suffix *-ible* creates an

adjective. If someone's handwriting is **illegible,** what words would you use to describe it?

_____

Dictionary definition _____

**EXERCISE B** **Prefixes**
**Words that begin with prefixes meaning "not" or "the opposite of" appear often in newspapers and magazines. Read an article. On a separate sheet of paper, make a list of the words you find containing the prefixes discussed in this lesson. After each word, use your vocabulary skills to make an educated guess about its meaning. Then, use a dictionary to write a definition of the word.**

# *Vocabulary Power*

## Lesson 9  Using Reading Skills
### Learning from Context: Definition

The context of a word is the environment, or the setting, in which it appears. You can use the context to discover the meaning of an unknown vocabulary word. Look for key words elsewhere in the sentence that will help you define the unknown word. Sometimes, other words in the sentence will provide a definition, or meaning, of the unknown word.

**EXERCISE**

**Use context to find the meaning of the boldfaced word. Underline key words in the sentence that help you define the unknown word. Then, write the boldfaced word's probable meaning on the line.**

1. My sister is a true **optimist;** no matter how dark the situation seems, she can always look on the

   bright side! _____

2. Author Jane Austen wrote **topical** novels based on the events of her day. _____

   _____

3. Hannah's **spontaneous** reaction to winning the first prize—her natural, genuine, and uncontrolled

   whoop—delighted everyone in the audience. _____

4. The **abstract** nature of the candidate's answers did not satisfy the listeners; they wanted to hear

   solid, concrete proposals. _____

5. By rejecting the laws of his society, the angry man became a **renegade.** _____

   _____

6. After dodging bullets, bombs, and hand grenades for the entire night, the messenger arrived at

   central headquarters **unscathed.** _____

7. Even though the shipwrecked survivors drank only a few drops of fresh water a day, their precious

   supply began to **dwindle.** _____

8. The large **throng** grew angrier and angrier; then, someone threw a rock at the president's carriage,

   and the crowd exploded in rage. _____

9. The politician was so **portly** he had trouble fitting into the chair. _____

   _____

10. Nothing at all grew in the **barren** soil; a treeless wasteland stretched as far as the eye could see.

   _____

# Vocabulary Power

## Review: Unit 2

**EXERCISE**

**Circle the word in parentheses that best completes each sentence.**

1. Because the bell had not yet rung, the teacher took the (opportunity, malfunction, status) to repeat her instructions.

2. Our senator decided to (align, oppose, detach) the bill because she believed it would place an unfair burden on the poor.

3. When traveling in some foreign countries, I have difficulty making the people (assert, vary, comprehend) what I am trying to say.

4. "It is my firm (dignity, conviction, antidote)," said the candidate, "that family farms must receive government help."

5. To enter the contest, just (detach, comprehend, assert) the coupon from the cereal box and mail it before the deadline.

6. Unlike the feathers of the brightly colored male cardinal, the feathers of the female are quite (passive, wily, drab).

7. Jason quickly read the bottle's label, searching for the proper (status, antidote, dignity) for the poison.

8. Mara looked completely (versatile, disoriented, obsessed) when we all yelled, "Surprise!" as she entered the house.

9. The (incompetent, wily, bewildered) captain created a clever plan of attack that was sure to confuse the enemy.

10. An air bag is a (hardy, drab, passive) form of protection; unlike a seat belt, you don't have to do anything to make it work.

*Vocabulary Power*

## Test: Unit 2

**PART A**

**Circle the letter of the word that best completes each sentence.**

1. The posters in Brian's room convinced me he was almost _____ with soccer.
   **a.** bewildered     **b.** incompetent     **c.** obsessed     **d.** spontaneous

2. Because our weather is cool, we have to buy _____ plants that don't freeze easily.
   **a.** hardy     **b.** wily     **c.** drab     **d.** abstract

3. The man was taken into custody because of his _____ behavior.
   **a.** versatile     **b.** irrational     **c.** passive     **d.** unabridged

4. The political party was having a hard time finding a candidate to _____ the popular incumbent from the other party.
   **a.** clarify     **b.** detach     **c.** oppose     **d.** align

5. You should have seen the look of _____ on Dad's face when he took the assemble-it-yourself bookcase out of the box.
   **a.** perplexity     **b.** conviction     **c.** status     **d.** bias

6. You'll have a better chance of finding that unusual word if you look it up in an _____ dictionary.
   **a.** unabridged     **b.** incompetent     **c.** illegible     **d.** irrational

7. The chipmunk at the campsite was so _____ that it had no trouble stealing food from us.
   **a.** disoriented     **b.** obsessed     **c.** wily     **d.** incompetent

8. The candidate's refusal to reveal her running mate led to much _____.
   **a.** malfunction     **b.** speculation     **c.** conviction     **d.** status

9. If you feel your point of view is right, then _____ your position to the committee.
   **a.** oppose     **b.** assert     **c.** comprehend     **d.** detach

10. Because the computer started to _____, all of the envelopes were addressed incorrectly.
    **a.** malfunction     **b.** preview     **c.** clarify     **d.** dwindle

# Vocabulary Power continued

Copyright © by The McGraw-Hill Companies, Inc.

## PART B

**Circle the letter of the expression that best answers the question.**

1. If you are right-handed and write with your left hand (or vice versa), which word might describe the result?
   a. illegible        b. irrational        c. drab        d. unabridged

2. What word would you use to describe someone who accepts bad things that happen without reacting to them?
   a. unabridged       b. passive           c. wily        d. illegible

3. Which of the following is a safe place for birds?
   a. an opportunity   b. an antidote       c. a sanctuary d. a bias

4. Which word would best describe an indecisive person?
   a. abstract         b. portly            c. noncommittal d. drab

5. How would you describe the shapes of cars available?
   a. They assert.     b. They vary.        c. They detach.  d. They malfunction.

## PART C

**Circle the letter of the word that is most nearly a synonym for, or means almost the same as, the boldfaced expression.**

1. prejudice
   a. bias        b. status        c. perplexity    d. dignity

2. confused
   a. versatile   b. passive       c. disoriented   d. obsessed

3. safety
   a. antidote    b. nonsense      c. sanctuary     d. status

4. unskillful
   a. irrational  b. incompetent   c. illegible     d. disoriented

5. make even
   a. align       b. detach        c. assert        d. vary

Vocabulary Power

*Vocabulary Power*

## Lesson 10  Using Synonyms

You improve your sports skills by stretching yourself and by challenging yourself to be a better player. Life is like that too. Only by challenging yourself can you grow and improve as a person.

**Word List**

| | | | |
|---|---|---|---|
| assess | loom | pitfall | undermine |
| eerie | momentary | pursue | zest |
| gauge | outpost | | |

### EXERCISE A  Synonyms

**Each boldfaced word below is paired with a synonym whose meaning you probably know. Think of words related to the synonym and write them on the line provided. Then, look up the word in a dictionary and write its meaning.**

1. **pitfall** : hidden danger _____

   Dictionary definition _____

2. **pursue** : chase _____

   Dictionary definition _____

3. **momentary** : short _____

   Dictionary definition _____

4. **eerie** : weird _____

   Dictionary definition _____

5. **gauge** : measure _____

   Dictionary definition _____

6. **zest** : excitement _____

   Dictionary definition _____

7. **undermine** : weaken _____

   Dictionary definition _____

8. **loom** : appear _____

   Dictionary definition _____

# Vocabulary Power *continued*

9. **outpost** : settlement _____

   Dictionary definition _____

10. **assess** : examine _____

   Dictionary definition _____

## EXERCISE B  Multiple-Meaning Words

**Many words in English have more than one meaning. Each meaning, however, is based on the meaning of the word root. The word *gauge*, for example, comes from the Late or Low Latin *gaugia* ("the standard measure of a cask") to the Old North French *gauge* ("a gauge") and, eventually, through the Middle English *gauge* ("a standard of measurement") to the present form. A dictionary entry for *gauge* will list many different meanings, but all of them are related to the root meaning, "a standard measure." Use a dictionary to help you write the precise definition of *gauge* as it is used in each sentence below.**

1. The engineer obtained a **gauge** of the distance between the railroad rails.

   Definition _____

2. Surveys can provide a reliable **gauge** of public opinion on most issues.

   Definition _____

3. The **gauge** indicated that the steam pressure was rising to a dangerous level.

   Definition _____

4. Experienced detectives can usually estimate the **gauge** of a shotgun barrel's diameter.

   Definition _____

5. Manufacturers of plastic household wrap use a common **gauge** of film thickness.

   Definition _____

6. Flying without use of the radio, the pilot tried to **gauge** the distance to the airport.

   Definition _____

7. The inspector's specifications helped her **gauge** the school's adherence to fire regulations.

   Definition _____

# Vocabulary Power

## Lesson 11  Using Synonyms

Have you ever had to overcome a challenge? Maybe the challenge you overcame was one that pushed you to grow a bit. Maybe you solved a problem and learned a new skill along the way. Other challenges await you. Overcoming challenges can also teach you about yourself. The words in this lesson are useful in examining and facing challenges.

**Word List**

| | | | |
|---|---|---|---|
| citadel | pinnacle | symbol | vigor |
| frenzy | restore | tranquil | vital |
| ominous | shun | | |

**EXERCISE A** **Synonyms**

Each boldfaced word below is paired with a synonym whose meaning you probably know. Think of other words related to the synonym and write them on the line provided. Then, look up the word in a dictionary and write its meaning.

1. **vigor** : strength _____

  Dictionary definition _____

2. **pinnacle** : top _____

  Dictionary definition _____

3. **citadel** : fortress _____

  Dictionary definition _____

4. **ominous** : threatening _____

  Dictionary definition _____

5. **frenzy** : wild excitement _____

  Dictionary definition _____

6. **vital** : alive _____

  Dictionary definition _____

7. **tranquil** : calm _____

  Dictionary definition _____

# Vocabulary Power *continued*

8. **symbol** : representation _____

   Dictionary definition _____

9. **shun** : avoid _____

   Dictionary definition _____

10. **restore** : bring back _____

   Dictionary definition _____

## EXERCISE B  Sentence Completion
**Write the word that best completes the sentence.**

1. We chose the panther as our _____ because of its great strength.

2. The moonlight shining on the quiet lake created a _____ feeling.

3. The doctor checked the patient's _____ signs and frowned.

4. When the rock star finally walked onto the stage, the crowd went into a _____.

5. It took the electric company twelve hours to _____ power after the storm.

6. The other squirrels seemed to _____ the one with the broken leg.

7. The storm clouds looked _____ as we raced back to the tent.

8. The mountain climbers cheered when they reached the rocky _____.

9. The flowers by the garage have a lot of _____, but the ones under the tree look scraggly.

10. My little brother thinks his room is his _____ where he is protected from the rest of us.

*Vocabulary Power*

## Lesson 12  Greek Word Roots

Knowing the meanings of Greek roots can help you make an educated guess about the meaning of a new word. Sometimes, however, the exact meaning of the new word isn't clear from the root. In this lesson, you'll learn ten useful English words that are based on roots from the Greek language.

---

**Word List**

| | | | |
|---|---|---|---|
| anarchy | dynamic | hydroelectric | synchronize |
| chronic | dynasty | monarch | tripod |
| chronicle | hydrant | | |

---

**EXERCISE A**  **Word Origins**
**Read the clues. Then, answer the questions.**

1. *Chron, chrono* is a Greek root meaning "time." Adding the adjective suffix *-ic* makes a word that is often used to describe diseases. What do you think a **chronic** disease is?

   _____

2. The prefix *syn-* comes from a Greek word and means "with" or "together." The suffix *-ize* creates a verb form. If two people **synchronize** their watches, what are they doing?

   _____

3. Another English word based on this Greek root is **chronicle**, a story, usually of a historical event. How would you guess the events in a **chronicle** are presented?

   _____

4. The Greek root *hydr, hydro* means "water." The suffix *-ant* is used to create a noun. What comes out of a **hydrant**? Why is the most common type of hydrant called a fire hydrant?

   _____

5. Much electric power is generated in plants that use coal, gasoline, or natural gas. Other electric power is created by wind or the sun's energy. How would you guess **hydroelectric** power is generated?

   _____

# Vocabulary Power continued

**6.** Another common Greek root, *arch, archy,* means "ruler" or "leader." The number prefix *mon-* means "one," "alone," or "single." Give an example of a **monarch.**

_____

**7.** *A-, an-* is a negative prefix meaning "not" or "without." How would you describe conditions in a country where **anarchy** is present?

_____

**8.** A Greek root that means "power" or "force" is *dyn, dyna.* Adding an adjective suffix *-ic* to this root creates the English adjective **dynamic,** which probably means what?

_____

**9.** Adding the noun suffix *-asty* to the root *dyn* creates another word. If someone is a member of a **dynasty,** how might you describe him or her?

_____

**10.** A common Greek root is *pod,* which means "foot." If a triangle has three angles, how many feet does a **tripod** have? What is a common use for a tripod?

_____

## EXERCISE B Word Web

**On a separate sheet of paper, make two copies of the word web shown below. Choose two of the Greek roots discussed in this lesson. Write one of the roots in the center of each circle. Then, add as many words as you can with the same Greek root. Quiz a partner about the meanings of the words you add to your webs.**

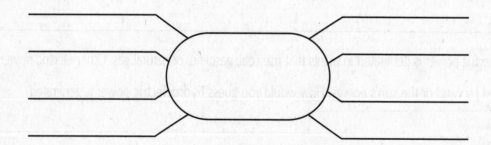

# Vocabulary Power

## Lesson 13  Suffixes That Form Nouns

A suffix is a word ending that can be added to a word or root. Adding a suffix changes the word's meaning. It can also change the word's part of speech from, for example, a noun to a verb. Some common suffixes that change a word or root to a noun are *-or, -er, -age, -ism, -tion,* and *-ation.* In this lesson, you'll explore how noun suffixes are used to create noun forms from different words.

### Word List

| | | | |
|---|---|---|---|
| advantage | condemnation | spoilage | termination |
| aviator | investor | temptation | vendor |
| communism | realism | | |

### EXERCISE A  Word Clues

**Use the clues given to answer the questions.**

1. To invest means to give money for the purpose of making a profit.

   What is an **investor?** _____

2. *Vend* is an old word that means "to sell." What does a hot dog **vendor** do?

   _____

3. Aviation is the science of flying airplanes. What would you guess is the job of an **aviator?**

   _____

4. If something spoils, it is no longer fit for use. How would you define the noun **spoilage?**

   _____

5. To advance is to move forward. Adding a noun suffix to the root *advance* creates **advantage,**

   which probably means _____

6. To be realistic means to be practical, concerned about the facts, or willing to see things as they are.

   What are some words that might be synonyms for the noun form **realism?**

   _____

7. A communist believes that all the people should benefit equally from the factories, farms, and

   businesses that make up a country's economy. How would you describe **communism?**

   _____

# Vocabulary Power *continued*

8. The verb *condemn* means to declare something to be wrong or evil. What is your definition of the

   noun **condemnation**? _____

9. The Latin root *temptare* means "to feel" or "to try." A **temptation** usually refers to being enticed

   into doing something wrong. Give an example of a temptation. _____

   _____

10. To terminate something is to end it. How would you define the noun **termination**?

    _____

## EXERCISE B  Definitions
**Look up each word in a dictionary. Write the definition on the line provided.**

1. investor _____

2. vendor _____

3. aviator _____

4. spoilage _____

5. advantage _____

6. realism _____

7. communism _____

8. condemnation _____

9. temptation _____

10. termination _____

*Vocabulary Power*

## Lesson 14 Using Reference Skills
### Using a Thesaurus: Synonyms
A thesaurus is a useful reference work that lists synonyms (and often antonyms) for thousands of words. The synonyms vary slightly in meaning and feeling, and the listing is designed to help you choose just the right word. To use a thesaurus, you must look in the index for the word for which you want to find synonyms. A number refers you to a listing in the main part of the thesaurus. In this lesson, you'll practice using a thesaurus to find synonyms.

**EXERCISE**

**Look over the thesaurus entries below. Then, answer the questions.**

> **96 appalling** *adj.* dreadful, fearful, horrible, awful, ghastly, frightening, horrendous, hateful, shocking, icky, spooky, terrifying, creepy
>
> **207 illuminate** *v.* clear up, explain, enlighten, illustrate, picture, portray, reveal, show, clarify
>
> **819 traumatic** *adj.* damaging, disabling, disturbing, jolting, shocking, upsetting, mind-boggling

1. Which synonyms for **appalling** might you use if you were writing a ghost story?

   _____

   If you were writing a news report about a crime? _____

   Explain your answers. _____

   _____

2. Which synonym for **traumatic** seems to you to be the strongest in its feeling? Explain your answer.

   _____

   Which seems the mildest? _____

3. Suppose you are having trouble deciding whether to use *clarify* or *illustrate* as a synonym for

   **illuminate.** How would you find out exactly how the two words differ in meaning?

   _____

4. **Traumatic** appears here as an adjective. Look at the adjectives given as synonyms. Change the

   form of those adjectives to write synonyms for the noun *trauma.* (For example, from the adjective

   *damaging,* you would write the noun *damage.*)

   _____

*Vocabulary Power*

## Review: Unit 3

**EXERCISE**

**Circle the word in parentheses that best completes each sentence.**

1. It took the arrival of three police cars to (undermine, restore, shun) order at the scene.

2. Cheyenne learned about the (termination, advantage, vigor) of her library privileges when the computer refused to renew her library card because of unpaid fines.

3. The governor harshly blamed the mayor for trying to (shun, undermine, gauge) support for the new prison.

4. The setting was (dynamic, tranquil, vital)—calm winds, a clear sky, and many stars.

5. My grandfather has trouble walking because of the (chronic, vital, dynamic) pain in his knees from playing football in college.

6. The movie was about the exciting life of a daredevil (investor, vendor, aviator) in the 1920s and the self-constructed airplanes he flew.

7. The announcement that a movie would be filmed in our town sent everyone into a (pitfall, temptation, frenzy).

8. The photographer set the camera on a special (hydrant, tripod, chronicle) and then asked the couple to smile.

9. Before we can say whether the bike is usable, we'll have to (pursue, chronicle, assess) the damage from the accident.

10. This planning committee could use someone with a strong sense of (realism, communism, anarchy) so our ideas don't get too off the wall!

Name _____  Date _____  Class _____

 *Vocabulary Power*

## Test: Unit 3

**PART A**

**Circle the letter of the word that best completes the sentence.**

1. The firefighters connected the hose to the nearest _____.
   a. vendor       b. outpost       c. hydrant       d. pitfall

2. Because the hikers planned to reunite at 4:00 P.M., they paused to _____ their watches.
   a. assess       b. synchronize   c. restore       d. shun

3. The rumble of thunder in the distance sounded _____, and I feared we would not reach the cabin before the storm.
   a. ominous      b. chronic       c. tranquil      d. vital

4. Mom was trying to find a(n) _____ to help finance her printing business.
   a. aviator      b. investor      c. dynasty       d. monarch

5. Getting this blood to the accident victims is absolutely _____!
   a. eerie        b. chronic       c. dynamic       d. vital

6. The mountain seemed to _____ larger and larger as I approached.
   a. pursue       b. restore       c. loom          d. synchronize

7. Those playful puppies have a _____ for life that always makes me laugh.
   a. pinnacle     b. symbol        c. zest          d. spoilage

8. The new dam will supply _____ power to several towns and cities in the valley.
   a. ominous      b. hydrant       c. chronic       d. hydroelectric

9. The flag is a _____ of our country.
   a. symbol       b. outpost       c. dynasty       d. frenzy

10. How you deal with a _____ in life says much about your character.
    a. pitfall     b. citadel       c. chronicle     d. monarch

11. The mayor warned that the city would be reduced to _____ if the police went on strike.
    a. condemnation  b. communism   c. termination   d. anarchy

12. Queen Elizabeth of Great Britain is probably the world's most famous _____.
    a. symbol      b. monarch       c. dynasty       d. citadel

13. The man waiting to see you is a _____ of office supplies and equipment.
    a. chronicle   b. frenzy        c. vendor        d. tripod

# Vocabulary Power continued

14. Because of the large amount of _____ in the supply of harvested corn and potatoes, many people in the village will go hungry this winter.

   **a.** pitfall          **b.** spoilage          **c.** vigor          **d.** realism

15. *Little Women* by Louisa May Alcott is the _____ of a lively New England family in the 1800s.

   **a.** dynasty          **b.** termination          **c.** chronicle          **d.** pinnacle

## PART B

**Circle the letter of the word that is most nearly the *opposite* of the boldfaced word.**

1. **welcome**
   **a.** pursue          **b.** shun          **c.** loom          **d.** gauge

2. **feeble**
   **a.** ominous          **b.** momentary          **c.** dynamic          **d.** chronic

3. **order**
   **a.** zest          **b.** condemnation          **c.** spoilage          **d.** anarchy

4. **flee**
   **a.** shun          **b.** pursue          **c.** gauge          **d.** loom

5. **weakness**
   **a.** vigor          **b.** spoilage          **c.** pitfall          **d.** zest

## PART C

**Circle the letter of the word or words that best answers the question.**

1. Which word comes from a military source?
   **a.** pinnacle          **b.** pitfall          **c.** dynasty          **d.** outpost

2. What would most dieters consider a hot fudge sundae to be?
   **a.** a temptation          **b.** an advantage          **c.** a termination          **d.** a spoilage

3. Which type of person could tell you city airport abbreviations?
   **a.** monarch          **b.** aviator          **c.** vendor          **d.** anarchist

4. What is used to measure air pressure in a tire?
   **a.** tripod          **b.** symbol          **c.** gauge          **d.** outpost

5. If you bought an abandoned building, what would you try to do?
   **a.** synchronize it          **b.** restore it          **c.** undermine it          **d.** weigh it

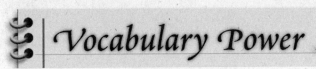

# Vocabulary Power

## Lesson 15  Word Usage

When you think of "home," what do you think of? A private space to call your own? Brothers and sisters to laugh and argue with? A place of safety and understanding? The words in this list can be used to describe feelings about home.

**Word List**

| | | | |
|---|---|---|---|
| anticipation | exuberant | obscure | refuge |
| compassion | indifferent | perilous | relinquish |
| confront | nurture | | |

### EXERCISE A  Sentence Completion

**Write the vocabulary word that best completes each sentence. Use a dictionary if necessary.**

1. At dawn the fog may _____ the beautiful suspension bridge, so we should take a picture now.

2. The ticket takers at the movie theater will _____ anyone who tries to sneak in without a ticket.

3. In a state of _____, the whole family was excitedly counting down the days until Carrie's wedding.

4. I'd like to get a closer look at that eagle soaring in the sky, but Marty will not _____ the binoculars.

5. The bluebird parents _____ their babies until the babies can fly and feed themselves.

6. During the _____ ocean voyage, the travelers faced storms, fire, and lack of food.

7. Reaching out to comfort and care for others shows that you have _____.

8. The _____ children joyously ripped open their presents on Christmas morning.

9. Camryn was excited about visiting the White House, but Jake appeared _____ to the whole experience.

10. Where should I seek _____ in case of a storm?

# Vocabulary Power *continued*

## EXERCISE B  Usage
**Write the vocabulary word that could describe each example.**

1. a dogsled journey across broken ice in the Arctic          _____

2. a cheerleader performing at a pep rally          _____

3. attitude of someone who doesn't care who wins an election          _____

4. pond and surrounding land where ducks and other birds are not hunted _____

5. desire to help war victims suffering from a lack of food and supplies          _____

## EXERCISE C  Usage
**Draw a line through the italicized word or phrase. Above it, write the vocabulary word that can replace the word or phrase.**

1. Through clear instruction and careful application, a teacher learns to *develop the potential of* each student.

2. When we *meet* difficulties head-on, we exercise decision-making and problem-solving skills.

3. World leaders demanded that the dictator *release* his hold on the helpless country.

4. The candidate made a(n) *vague* reference to his opponent's political past.

5. In *looking forward*, the designer decorated the store windows for the holiday.

6. The ship rode out the *dangerous* seas without incident.

7. Many travelers sought *shelter* in the country inn from the sudden storm.

8. Out of *pity* for the accident victim, the bystander covered him with a blanket.

9. The teen's *unenthusiastic* attitude in class masked his insecurity about math.

10. Television cameras recorded her *joyously unrestrained* response to the election outcome.

# Vocabulary Power

## Lesson 16  Using Context Clues

Storytellers capture their listeners and readers through language that suggests mystery, intrigue, romance, and other human experiences. Words such as *murky, ravenous,* and *scour* build suspense and trigger the imagination. The list below should invite you to explore word imagery.

**Word List**

| | | | |
|---|---|---|---|
| beneficial | crucial | murky | ravenous |
| compensation | devise | premonition | scour |
| consolation | dispense | | |

**EXERCISE A**  Context Clues

**Use context clues to guess the meaning of the boldfaced word. Then, look up the word in a dictionary and write its meaning.**

1. Bernice will **devise** a system for recycling plastic containers.

   My definition _____

   Dictionary definition _____

2. The water in the pond was too **murky** to see the fish.

   My definition _____

   Dictionary definition _____

3. A good detective will **scour** the scene of the crime for clues.

   My definition _____

   Dictionary definition _____

4. These machines **dispense** crackers and other snacks.

   My definition _____

   Dictionary definition _____

5. The vitamins in fruits and vegetables are **beneficial** to your health.

   My definition _____

   Dictionary definition _____

6. The ringing phone confirmed Julia's **premonition** that Mark might call today.

   My definition _____

   Dictionary definition _____

# Vocabulary Power *continued*

**7.** The **ravenous** hikers had not eaten for two days.

My definition _____

Dictionary definition _____

**8.** Erin's kindness was a **consolation** to Jessica, who was alone in a new country.

My definition _____

Dictionary definition _____

**9.** Katrina scored the **crucial** goal that brought her soccer team to victory.

My definition _____

Dictionary definition _____

**10.** Brent gave Mr. Wu ten dollars as **compensation** for the window he broke.

My definition _____

Dictionary definition _____

## EXERCISE B  Sentence Completion
**Circle the word that correctly completes each sentence.**

**1.** If the weather is hot for the county fair, volunteers will (devise, scour, dispense) ice water.

**2.** Building strong bones is one of the (beneficial, ravenous, crucial) effects of drinking milk.

**3.** Knowing that he had done his best was (consolation, premonition, crucial) for losing the race.

**4.** The (murky, crucial, ravenous) guests devoured the chocolate cake in five minutes.

## EXERCISE C  Clues Matching
**Write the word that matches each definition.**

**1.** dark or dim _____

**4.** payment for a loss _____

**2.** forewarning _____

**5.** search thoroughly _____

**3.** create _____

**6.** having a positive effect _____

## EXERCISE D  Multiple-Meaning Words
**Look up the word *dispense* in a dictionary. Note that *dispense* has several different meanings. On a separate sheet of paper, write a sentence for each definition, using the word correctly.**

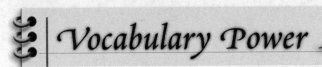

# Vocabulary Power

## Lesson 17 Prefixes That Tell When

A prefix is a word part attached at the beginning of a word or root. The prefix *pre-* means "before" and the prefix *post-* means "after." Adding a prefix to a word or root modifies its meaning. For example, the word *prequalify* means "qualify beforehand," and the word *postgame* means "after the game." Recognizing these two prefixes that tell when can often help you figure out a word's meaning.

---

**Word List**

| | | | |
|---|---|---|---|
| posterity | preamble | predetermine | prerequisite |
| postscript | preconceived | premature | presume |
| postseason | predate | | |

---

**EXERCISE A**   **Words and Word Roots**

**Use the meaning of the prefix and the information given about the base word or root to arrive at a possible meaning for each word. Then, look up the word in a dictionary and write its definition.**

1. *Conceived* means "thought of." **Preconceived** might mean

   _____

   Dictionary definition _____

2. One meaning of *season* is "the time of year when a sport is played." **Postseason** might mean

   _____

   Dictionary definition _____

3. *Date* can mean "to occur at a certain time." **Predate** might mean

   _____

   Dictionary definition _____

4. *Script* refers to something written. **Postscript** might mean

   _____

   Dictionary definition _____

5. *Mature* can mean "ripe." **Premature** might mean

   _____

   Dictionary definition _____

# Vocabulary Power *continued*

**6.** A *requisite* is something that is required. **Prerequisite** might mean

_____

Dictionary definition _____

**7.** The root *sumere* means "take." **Presume** might mean

_____

Dictionary definition _____

**8.** The Latin *posterus* means "coming after." **Posterity** might mean

_____

Dictionary definition _____

**9.** *Determine* means "decide" or "establish." **Predetermine** might mean

_____

Dictionary definition _____

**10.** The root *ambulare* means "walk." **Preamble** might mean

_____

Dictionary definition _____

**EXERCISE B** Word Association
## Write the vocabulary word that could describe each example.

1. a tomato picked while it is still hard and green _____

2. playoff game used to determine a champion _____

3. message saying "Don't be late" after the signature on a letter _____

4. being at least five feet tall in order to ride a roller coaster _____

5. a paragraph at the beginning of a treaty explaining its purpose _____

6. belief formed about something before evaluating the facts _____

7. people not yet born who will view today's current events as history _____

8. decide ahead of time what food you will order at a restaurant _____

9. events during the American Revolution in reference to the Civil War _____

10. what a jury must do about a person's innocence until guilt is proved _____

*Vocabulary Power*

## Lesson 18  Using Reference Skills

**Using a Dictionary: Word Origins**

Most dictionary entries include a brief note about the word's origin, or beginning. The word origin usually appears in brackets at the beginning or end of the entry. Here are several examples.

> **behemoth** (bi hē′ məth) *n.*  Something huge in size or power [From Hebrew *behemoth,* a huge beast, possibly a hippopotamus, mentioned in the Old Testament of the Bible.]
>
> **maverick** (mav′ er ik) *n.* **1.** An unbranded range animal, especially a calf that has become separated from its mother **2.** An independent person who does not go along with the group [Probably from Samuel August Maverick (1803–1870), a Texas cattleman who did not brand his calves.]
>
> **tantalize** (tan′ tə līz) *v.* To excite or tease by presenting something desirable that is out of reach [From Latin *Tantalus,* a mythological Greek king who was punished for his crimes by having to stand, hungry and thirsty, in water that drew away when he tried to drink it and beneath hanging fruit that drew away when he reached for it.]

**EXERCISE**

**Use the sample entries above to answer each question about word origins.**

1. Which word comes from the Hebrew language?

_____

What did this word originally refer to?

_____

2. Which word comes from the name of a mythological king?

_____

When something tantalizes you, how are you like that king?

_____

3. What is the origin of the word *maverick?*

_____

How does the second meaning of this word relate to the word origin?

_____

# Vocabulary Power

## Review: Unit 4

**EXERCISE**

**Circle the word in parentheses that correctly completes each sentence.**

1. Janet decided to (nurture, scour, obscure) the city to find the perfect present for her sister.

2. Will you receive some (consolation, compensation, premonition) for your summer job, or are you working as a volunteer?

3. On-time delivery of packages is (premature, crucial, murky) during the busy holiday season.

4. As part of a national park, the Grand Canyon will be preserved for (preamble, posterity, refuge).

5. Larry has some (perilous, preconceived, beneficial) ideas about what the Netherlands is like, but he has never been there.

6. Did the first Egyptian dynasty (predate, predetermine, relinquish) the Holy Roman Empire?

7. At the aquarium, the (indifferent, exuberant, premature) children squealed with delight as they watched the playful sea otters.

8. The volleyball players took (refuge, compassion, anticipation) from the storm in a picnic shelter.

9. Is understanding negative numbers a (preamble, prerequisite, postscript) for taking algebra?

10. Nicholas will (dispense, relinquish, nurture) pencils and others supplies to the students as they enter the room.

11. We look forward to your speech with (anticipation, premonition, compassion)!

12. Denise is well-known as a collector of (ravenous, indifferent, obscure) artifacts from Asia.

13. He decided to (presume, confront, nurture) his secretary about the stolen money.

14. Without your input, we will have to (devise, scour, presume) that our results are correct.

15. The lake was too (murky, preconceived, beneficial) for me to swim today.

*Vocabulary Power*

## Test: Unit 4

### PART A

**Circle the letter of the word that best completes the sentence.**

**1.** In summer the leafy trees will _____ the tourists' view of the castle.
   **a.** scour       **b.** confront       **c.** obscure       **d.** dispense

**2.** Out of _____, the nun set up a free hospital for the poor in India.
   **a.** compensation    **b.** compassion       **c.** posterity       **d.** consolation

**3.** Leroy looks forward to horsemanship events at the fair with great _____.
   **a.** anticipation     **b.** preamble       **c.** premonition       **d.** refuge

**4.** We need to _____ a plan that will get us out of this maze!
   **a.** presume       **b.** nurture       **c.** predate       **d.** devise

**5.** Jeremy will _____ the library shelves to find a biography of Sojourner Truth.
   **a.** scour       **b.** obscure       **c.** predate       **d.** presume

**6.** Kristin's _____ ideas about older people disappeared after she met Mr. Jensen, a seventy-year-old man who runs marathons.
   **a.** preconceived    **b.** premature       **c.** crucial       **d.** perilous

**7.** At this school, taking a writing course is a _____ for taking drama.
   **a.** compensation    **b.** postscript       **c.** premonition       **d.** prerequisite

**8.** You need to _____ this problem instead of pretending it doesn't exist!
   **a.** relinquish       **b.** confront       **c.** predetermine       **d.** presume

**9.** Judy will _____ the plant until it is healthy again.
   **a.** devise       **b.** nurture       **c.** presume       **d.** scour

**10.** Although Tim was injured in the second quarter, it was a _____ that his team won.
   **a.** consolation       **b.** postseason       **c.** posterity       **d.** prerequisite

### PART B

**Write the letter of the word that has the same meaning as the boldfaced expression.**

**1. full of joy or enthusiasm**
   **a.** ravenous       **b.** murky       **c.** perilous       **d.** exuberant

**2. distribute in portions**
   **a.** relinquish       **b.** dispense       **c.** predetermine       **d.** presume

3. future generations
   a. refuge      b. posterity      c. postscript      d. preamble

4. occurring too early
   a. crucial      b. preconceived      c. premature      d. postseason

5. payment for a loss or for a service
   a. compensation      b. postscript      c. consolation      d. anticipation

6. of great importance
   a. perilous      b. crucial      c. indifferent      d. exuberant

7. let go of
   a. devise      b. nurture      c. relinquish      d. scour

8. take for granted as true
   a. presume      b. relinquish      c. predetermine      d. confront

9. dangerous
   a. beneficial      b. crucial      c. murky      d. perilous

10. not strongly for or against
    a. ravenous      b. premature      c. indifferent      d. beneficial

11. establish ahead of time
    a. presume      b. predate      c. predetermine      d. dispense

12. occurring after the regular time when a sport is played
    a. premonition      b. prerequisite      c. postseason      d. postscript

13. feeling that something will occur
    a. compensation      b. premonition      c. consolation      d. compassion

14. message added at the end of a letter
    a. anticipation      b. posterity      c. postseason      d. postscript

15. helpful or advantageous
    a. indifferent      b. beneficial      c. murky      d. perilous

Name _____ Date _____ Class _____

 *Vocabulary Power*

## Lesson 19  Using Context Clues

Yogi Berra, a famous New York Yankee baseball player, once said, "When you come to a fork in the road, take it!" In life, a person must often choose one path or the other. The words in this list can help you write and talk about making choices.

**Word List**

| circumstance | frail | modest | ordeal |
|---|---|---|---|
| defiant | intimidated | nimble | resilient |
| desolate | mobility | | |

### EXERCISE A  Context Clues

**Each sentence below contains a clue about the meaning of the boldfaced word. Use the clue to guess the meaning of the word and write it on the first line. Then, look up the word in a dictionary and write its meaning.**

1. A **modest** hero would never brag. _____

   Dictionary definition _____

2. A **frail** fence might fall over easily. _____

   Dictionary definition _____

3. A **defiant** American patriot in 1775 might disobey British laws. _____

   Dictionary definition _____

4. A bully could make you feel **intimidated.** _____

   Dictionary definition _____

5. Recovering from a serious accident can be an **ordeal.** _____

   Dictionary definition _____

6. At 3:00 A.M., city streets look **desolate.** _____

   Dictionary definition _____

7. Good **mobility** is important in playing sports. _____

   Dictionary definition _____

8. A trampoline's surface is **resilient.** _____

   Dictionary definition _____

Copyright © by The McGraw-Hill Companies, Inc.

9. A **nimble** Jack jumped over the candlestick. _____

Dictionary definition _____

10. Heavy rain creates a risky **circumstance** for driving. _____

Dictionary definition _____

## EXERCISE B  Word Association
**For each group of words, write the vocabulary word that belongs.**

1. weak, fragile, flimsy _____

2. flexible, elastic, springy _____

3. quick, agile, skillful _____

4. disobedient, antagonistic, bold _____

5. unboastful, diffident, shy _____

## EXERCISE C  Usage
**Write the vocabulary word that can replace each italicized word or phrase.**

1. What *condition* caused Inez to postpone the party? _____

2. The *deserted* mining town was absolutely quiet except
for the sound of blowing wind. _____

3. The snowstorm that closed the highway was a(n) *difficult*
*experience* for travelers. _____

4. Andre has much more *ease of movement* now that
he has a motorized wheelchair. _____

5. The large bull in the field made us feel *fearful,* so we
decided not to climb over the fence. _____

## EXERCISE D  Crossword Puzzle
**With a partner, create a crossword puzzle that includes at least six of the vocabulary
words. Be sure to include the clues.**

# Vocabulary Power

## Lesson 20  Using Synonyms

What helps you when you have a tough decision to make? Do you consider the advice of friends and family? Do you think about principles, or rules for action, such as treating others fairly or not wasting resources? Do you weigh the pros and cons? The words in this list can help you consider decisions.

> **Word List**
>
> | | | | |
> |---|---|---|---|
> | acutely | drastically | mock | somberly |
> | collaborate | falter | soberly | surge |
> | displace | improvise | | |

### EXERCISE A  Synonyms

**Each boldfaced word is paired with a synonym whose meaning you probably know. Think of another related word and write it on the line provided. Then, look up the vocabulary word in a dictionary and write its meaning.**

1. **mock** : ridicule _____

   Dictionary definition _____

2. **collaborate** : cooperate _____

   Dictionary definition _____

3. **falter** : hesitate _____

   Dictionary definition _____

4. **soberly** : seriously _____

   Dictionary definition _____

5. **surge** : swell _____

   Dictionary definition _____

6. **drastically** : harshly _____

   Dictionary definition _____

7. **displace** : remove _____

   Dictionary definition _____

8. **somberly** : gloomily _____

   Dictionary definition _____

# Vocabulary Power continued

9. **acutely** : sharply _____

   Dictionary definition _____

10. **improvise** : invent _____

    Dictionary definition _____

## EXERCISE B  Adverbs
**Complete each sentence with the best adverb from the vocabulary list.**

1. Kyle _____ announced that he was moving to Chicago to live with his father.

2. Lottie is _____ sensitive to other people's feelings.

3. The bright orange paint _____ altered the appearance of the house.

4. Feeling as if he had no friends, Uri _____ reflected on his future.

## EXERCISE C  Questions and Answers
**Answer each question, using the meaning of the boldfaced word.**

1. If you came to a baseball game unprepared for the sun, how could you **improvise** a shade for

   your head or eyes? _____

2. If you saw a crowd **surge** into an auditorium, what would it look like? _____

   _____

3. How could the tennis player ranked second in the world **displace** the top-ranked player? _____

   _____

4. How do political cartoonists show they are **mocking** a politician? _____

   _____

5. How could two people **collaborate** on a surprise birthday party for a third person? _____

   _____

6. If you saw a tightrope walker **falter** in the middle of a performance, what would you notice? What

   feelings might he or she be having? _____

   _____

# Vocabulary Power

## Lesson 21  Latin Word Roots

Many English words have roots that come from Latin, the language spoken by the Romans. For example, the words *predict* and *dictionary* share the Latin root *dict,* which means "say." Recognizing Latin roots can often help you figure out the meaning of an unfamiliar word.

**Word List**

| | | | |
|---|---|---|---|
| advocate | documentation | resent | sentimental |
| aggravate | grave | revoke | version |
| docile | invert | | |

### EXERCISE A  Word Roots

**Write two words from the list for each root below. After the word, write its dictionary definition.**

*doc* (teach)

1. _____

2. _____

*sent* (feel)

3. _____

4. _____

*voc* (call, voice)

5. _____

6. _____

*grav* (heavy)

7. _____

8. _____

*vert, vers* (turn)

9. _____

10. _____

# Vocabulary Power *continued*

## EXERCISE B  Multiple-Meaning Words

**Use context clues to determine which meaning of the boldfaced word is used. Then, write the dictionary definition that applies.**

1. Mr. Krebs, a known cheater, is always caught in a **revoke** while playing cards.

   _____

2. The police can **revoke** your driver's license for reckless driving.

   _____

3. The modern English **version** of Homer's *Odyssey* has lost some of the original meaning.

   _____

4. The experimental **version** of the single-person glider will be tested tomorrow.

   _____

5. The **grave** procession, in which everyone was dressed in black, passed me by.

   _____

6. Her job at the shipyard was to **grave** each ship's keel and bottom.

   _____

7. The composer has marked this section of the composition **grave**, reminding orchestra members they are playing a funeral march.

   _____

8. The coffin of my Great Aunt Ginny was lowered into the open **grave**.

   _____

9. I need **documentation** for this fact so that I can use it in my speech.

   _____

10. Nancy didn't intend to **aggravate** her tendonitis, but her condition worsened as she continued to exercise.

   _____

# Vocabulary Power

## Lesson 22  Suffixes That Form Adjectives

A suffix is an ending that can be added to a word or root. Adding a suffix to a word or root often changes the word's part of speech. For example, when -able is added to the verb return, the adjective returnable is formed. Words ending in the suffixes listed below are always adjectives.

| Suffix | Meaning | Example |
|---|---|---|
| -able | able or capable of | dependable (depend + able) |
| -al | of or relating to | personal (person + al) |
| -ic | of or relating to | angelic (angel + ic) |
| -ive | tending to | creative (create + ive) |
| -y | have the character of; like; showing | grimy (grime + y) |

### Word List

| academic | despicable | lamentable | lofty |
|---|---|---|---|
| annual | distinctive | lethal | primary |
| civic | inquisitive | | |

### EXERCISE A  Suffixes

Write two adjectives from the list for each suffix below. After the word, write its dictionary definition.

*-ic*

1. _____

2. _____

*-al*

3. _____

4. _____

*-ive*

5. _____

6. _____

*-able*

7. _____

8. _____

# Vocabulary Power *continued*

-y

9. _____

10. _____

**EXERCISE B** **Context Clues**
**Write the vocabulary word that could describe each example.**

1. a horrifying act _____

2. a mountain peak hidden by clouds _____

3. the shattering of people's lives by an earthquake _____

4. the duty of serving on a jury _____

5. a flower that lasts for just one season _____

6. a main reason for doing something _____

7. a wound that causes an animal's death _____

8. clothing that makes you stand out from others _____

9. performance in your classes at school _____

10. a person who is thirsty for knowledge _____

**EXERCISE C** **Dictionary Definitions**
**Did you know that you can look up a suffix in a dictionary? Look up the suffixes -en and -ous. List an adjective that contains each suffix and write its meaning.**

1. _____

_____

2. _____

_____

# Vocabulary Power

## Lesson 23  Using Reading Skills
### Learning from Context: Examples

When you encounter a new word in your reading, you can often use the context, or the surrounding words, to figure out the word's meaning. Sometimes, the sentence includes clues about the meaning of the word, as in the following sentence:

The *spacious* apartment had a large bedroom, a living room big enough for our grand piano, and a kitchen with plenty of work space.

From the examples, you could figure out that *spacious* means "roomy."

### EXERCISE A

**In each sentence, circle the examples that help you understand the meaning of the boldfaced term. Then, write a possible definition of the word.**

1. The room has several sources of **illumination,** including table and floor lamps, and a large bay window.

    **Illumination** probably means _____.

2. The three friends stopped at a cafe to **imbibe** endless cups of coffee.

    **Imbibe** probably means _____.

3. Many companies are best known by their **acronyms,** such as IBM, for International Business Machines Corporation, and TWA, for Trans World Airlines.

    **Acronym** probably means _____.

4. This region has recently experienced a major **catastrophe**—an earthquake.

    **Catastrophe** probably means _____.

5. The menu listed freshly baked pies, German chocolate cake, and other **delectable** desserts.

    **Delectable** probably means _____.

6. Mr. Pardi enjoys pulling a good **prank;** one time, he caused quite a stir in the office by secretly replacing all the telephone receivers with bananas!

    **Prank** probably means _____.

### EXERCISE B

**Look up each boldfaced word from Exercise A in a dictionary. Rate the accuracy of your guess about the meaning of each word on a scale of 1 to 5, with 5 being most accurate.**

illumination _____      catastrophe _____      delectable _____

imbibe _____      acronym _____      prank _____

# Vocabulary Power

## Review: Unit 5

### EXERCISE A

**Circle the word that best completes each sentence.**

1. With her (acutely, somberly, drastically) sensitive ears, she heard the train coming from miles away.

2. The mayor and other (civic, academic, defiant) officials toured the water treatment plant.

3. Our club met with the principal to (aggravate, advocate, mock) more after-school programs.

4. During storms, water can (falter, surge, invert) onto the beach, so the homes are fortified.

5. The rising flood waters are creating a (grave, frail, resilient) situation for riverside residents.

6. Elena had not prepared an acceptance speech, so she had to (collaborate, aggravate, improvise).

7. The publisher predicts that the new novel will (invert, revoke, displace) the best-seller.

8. Cruelty to animals is at the top of her list of (despicable, primary, sentimental) behavior.

9. Trying out for the football team was a(n) (circumstance, ordeal, version) for Tony, who is small

   for his age.

10. When you cook chopped garlic in butter, a (distinctive, docile, desolate) aroma wafts in the kitchen.

### EXERCISE B

**Circle the word that is a synonym for the boldfaced word.**

1. **mobility**
   a. movement      b. payment      c. maintenance      d. sports

2. **displace**
   a. insult      b. lease      c. expel      d. lurk

3. **ordeal**
   a. meeting      b. flight      c. machine      d. trial

4. **falter**
   a. run      b. scatter      c. hesitate      d. shift

5. **docile**
   a. obedient      b. simple      c. modern      d. harsh

*Vocabulary Power*

## Test: Unit 5

**PART A**

**Circle the letter of the word that is a synonym of the boldfaced word.**

**1. springy**
   a. nimble      b. docile      c. lofty      d. lamentable

**2. noticeable**
   a. modest      b. distinctive      c. sentimental      d. defiant

**3. disobedient**
   a. annual      b. defiant      c. despicable      d. frail

**4. emotional**
   a. sentimental      b. desolate      c. distinctive      d. lethal

**5. ridicule**
   a. displace      b. falter      c. surge      d. mock

**6. weak**
   a. inquisitive      b. docile      c. frail      d. grave

**7. cancel**
   a. aggravate      b. revoke      c. advocate      d. invert

**8. cooperate**
   a. collaborate      b. resent      c. improvise      d. desolate

**9. fearful**
   a. grave      b. sentimental      c. despicable      d. intimidated

**10. intensely**
   a. soberly      b. drastically      c. somberly      d. acutely

**PART B**

**Circle the letter of the word that best completes the sentence.**

**1.** Grandpa found it _____ that he could no longer run long distances.
   a. lamentable      b. grave      c. distinctive      d. nimble

**2.** The political crisis will _____ thousands of people.
   a. advocate      b. invert      c. mock      d. displace

# Vocabulary Power *continued*

3. Andrew is _____ sensitive to criticism; Delia, in contrast, is indifferent.
   - **a.** somberly
   - **b.** soberly
   - **c.** acutely
   - **d.** drastically

4. The teacher gave each student time to tell his or her _____ of what had happened.
   - **a.** ordeal
   - **b.** primary
   - **c.** circumstance
   - **d.** version

5. If you _____ the fraction one half, you get the whole number two.
   - **a.** invert
   - **b.** revoke
   - **c.** advocate
   - **d.** falter

## PART C

**Choose the word or phrase that best completes each sentence.**

1. If you treat something soberly, your attitude is _____.
   - **a.** sad
   - **b.** serious
   - **c.** silly
   - **d.** casual

2. If a person's annual salary is $25,000, the person receives _____ .
   - **a.** $25,000 each year
   - **b.** $25,000 twice a year
   - **c.** $25,000 a month
   - **d.** $25,000 a week

3. If you falter while giving a speech, you become _____.
   - **a.** silent
   - **b.** loud
   - **c.** hesitant
   - **d.** demanding

4. Mobility refers to the ability to _____.
   - **a.** stand
   - **b.** create
   - **c.** think
   - **d.** move

5. People would be most likely to behave somberly at a _____.
   - **a.** pep rally
   - **b.** funeral
   - **c.** birthday party
   - **d.** graduation

# Vocabulary Power

## Lesson 24  Using Synonyms

Life doesn't always turn out as you expect, but life's surprises can be a source of pleasure as well as pain. Either way, unexpected experiences can help you understand who you are and what you care about. The words in this list relate to the twists and turns of life.

### Word List

| | | | |
|---|---|---|---|
| competent | precise | shrewd | uniform |
| obstinate | prosperous | toxic | unsightly |
| offensive | raucous | | |

### EXERCISE A  Synonyms

**Each boldfaced word is paired with a synonym whose meaning you probably know. Think of other words related to the synonym and write your ideas on the line provided. Then, look up the vocabulary word in a dictionary and write its meaning.**

1. **obstinate** : stubborn _____

   Dictionary definition _____

2. **uniform** : unvarying _____

   Dictionary definition _____

3. **unsightly** : ugly _____

   Dictionary definition _____

4. **offensive** : annoying _____

   Dictionary definition _____

5. **toxic** : poisonous _____

   Dictionary definition _____

6. **precise** : exact _____

   Dictionary definition _____

7. **competent** : capable _____

   Dictionary definition _____

8. **shrewd** : clever _____

   Dictionary definition _____

# Vocabulary Power continued

9. **raucous** : harsh _____

 Dictionary definition _____

10. **prosperous** : successful _____

 Dictionary definition _____

## EXERCISE B Sentence Completion
### Complete each sentence with the most appropriate vocabulary word.

1. The _____ junkyard was the eyesore of the neighborhood.

2. After months of practice, Maynard is now a(n) _____ free-throw shooter.

3. The chemical in this bug spray is _____ to most flying insects.

4. The leaves on this tree are _____; they are all the same size and shape.

5. The countryside was quiet except for the _____ sound of a few crows in the cornfield.

6. The _____ business owner created clever advertisements that made the

 company's product a household name.

7. The _____ location of City Hall is 16 South Main Street.

8. My sister never lets me borrow her jewelry; she is so _____!

9. The _____ farms in this area have well-kept houses and barns and abundant crops.

10. A(n) _____ odor was coming from the trash can.

# *Vocabulary Power*

## Lesson 25  Using Context Clues

Daily routines offer patterns for living that make people feel comfortable and secure. But if these patterns never change, boredom can be the result. The twists and turns of life, or the unexpected changes, can challenge people and make life more interesting.

**Word List**

| | | | |
|---|---|---|---|
| conceive | jest | restrain | squander |
| eventually | maneuver | simultaneously | thrive |
| intercept | moderately | | |

**EXERCISE A  Context Clues**

**Each sentence below contains a clue about the meaning of the boldfaced word. Use the clue to guess about the likely meaning of the word. Write your guess on the first line. Then, look up the word in a dictionary and write its meaning.**

1. The general will **maneuver** his troops toward the enemy's rear guard.

   My definition _____

   Dictionary definition _____

2. She's a beginner now, but **eventually** she will be an expert swimmer.

   My definition _____

   Dictionary definition _____

3. Erik was able to **intercept** the quarterback's pass and prevent a touchdown.

   My definition _____

   Dictionary definition _____

4. The fence around the yard will **restrain** their energetic dog.

   My definition _____

   Dictionary definition _____

5. Grass does not **thrive** in hot, dry weather.

   My definition _____

   Dictionary definition _____

## Vocabulary Power *continued*

6. I'm not eager for the job but I wouldn't turn it down; in other words, I'm **moderately** interested.

   My definition _____

   Dictionary definition _____

7. The two spacecraft were launched **simultaneously** at dawn.

   My definition _____

   Dictionary definition _____

8. The committee will **conceive** a plan for a new playground.

   My definition _____

   Dictionary definition _____

9. Those two like to **jest** with each other; I often see them laughing with and teasing each other.

   My definition _____

   Dictionary definition _____

10. Don't **squander** that money on junk food and movies; save it!

    My definition _____

    Dictionary definition _____

**EXERCISE B** **Definitions**
**Write the vocabulary word that matches each definition.**

1. hold back          _____

2. imagine            _____

3. grow well          _____

4. spend wastefully   _____

5. move into or out of position _____

6. stop or interrupt  _____

7. to a medium degree _____

8. act or speak jokingly _____

9. at the same time   _____

10. at some future time _____

# Vocabulary Power

## Lesson 26  Using Synonyms

A synonym is a word that has a similar meaning to another word. For example, the words *big, huge,* and *gigantic* are all synonyms for *large.* Knowing synonyms can give you options for words. For example, you might choose to say "elderly man" rather than "old man" if you want to show a respectful attitude.

Knowing antonyms for words is also helpful. An antonym is a word that means the opposite, or nearly the opposite, of another word. For example, *small, tiny,* and *minute* are all antonyms of *large.*

**Word List**

| | | | |
|---|---|---|---|
| ample | concise | prevail | remote |
| arid | foster | prudent | tactful |
| audacious | hinder | | |

### EXERCISE A  Synonyms

**One synonym is given for each word below. Think of other words related to the synonym and write your ideas on the line provided. Then, look up the word in a dictionary and write its meaning.**

1. **tactful** : polite _____

   Dictionary definition _____

2. **remote** : distant _____

   Dictionary definition _____

3. **concise** : brief _____

   Dictionary definition _____

4. **prudent** : wise _____

   Dictionary definition _____

5. **ample** : plentiful _____

   Dictionary definition _____

6. **hinder** : delay _____

   Dictionary definition _____

7. **audacious** : bold _____

   Dictionary definition _____

# Vocabulary Power *continued*

**8. foster** : promote _____

   Dictionary definition _____

**9. arid** : dry _____

   Dictionary definition _____

**10. prevail** : overcome _____

   Dictionary definition _____

## EXERCISE B  Antonyms

**Knowing the antonym of a word strengthens your understanding of the word's meaning. Write an antonym for each vocabulary word below.**

1. arid        _____        6. prudent   _____

2. ample       _____        7. hinder    _____

3. prevail     _____        8. concise   _____

4. tactful     _____        9. foster    _____

5. audacious   _____       10. remote    _____

## EXERCISE C  Sentence Completion

**Complete each sentence with the correct vocabulary word.**

1. A(n) _____ response to driving on icy roads is to reduce your speed.

2. Ida's parents are trying to _____ her artistic talent by art instruction.

3. Did the snowstorm _____ you in getting to your grandmother's house on time?

4. Our team is behind now, but in the end we will _____!

5. The _____ driver sped along the berm and then swerved back into traffic.

6. The _____ island is located more than two hundred miles off the Atlantic coast.

7. We have _____ food for the picnic; no one will go away hungry.

8. A(n) _____ coach can criticize a player's performance without making him feel bad.

9. Jane's reply to the question was short and _____.

10. You need to bring a lot of water when traveling in Death Valley—conditions are

    extremely _____!

# Vocabulary Power

## Lesson 27  Prefixes That Tell Where

A prefix is a word part added at the beginning of a word or root. The prefix changes the root's meaning. For example, the word *absorb (ab + sorb)* means "suck away." Some prefixes, such as *ab-*, *ad-*, *de-*, and *sym-*, tell where. The table below gives the meaning of each prefix and a word example.

| Prefix | Meaning | Example | Definition |
|---|---|---|---|
| *ab-* | away | abnormal | away from normal |
| *ad-* | to | admire | wonder at |
| *de-* | away, down | decompose | break down |
| *sym-* | with, together | symbiotic | living together |

### Word List

| | | | |
|---|---|---|---|
| abrupt | administer | dejected | sympathy |
| abstain | deduce | symmetrical | symphony |
| adjacent | degenerate | | |

### EXERCISE A  Prefixes

Write the words from the list that share the same prefix. Then, look up the meaning of each word in a dictionary and write its definition.

*ab-* (away)

1. _____

2. _____

*ad-* (to)

3. _____

4. _____

*de-* (away, down)

5. _____

6. _____

7. _____

*sym-* (with, together)

8. _____

9. _____

10. _____

*Vocabulary Power* continued

## EXERCISE B  Usage

**If the boldfaced word is used correctly in the sentence, write *correct* above it. If it is not, draw a line through it and write the correct vocabulary word above it.**

1. As we watched the news, we felt **symphony** for the homeless people whose houses were destroyed in the earthquake.

2. The people who live in the community will **administer** the new neighborhood safety program.

3. From the scattered trash and large pawprints in the mud, we were able to **abstain** that a bear had visited the campground.

4. After performing poorly at the dress rehearsal for the ballet concert, Elaine felt **dejected**.

5. Our apartment is **symmetrical** to the park, so we have a nice view of the trees and the fountain.

## EXERCISE C  Clues Matching

**Write the word that could describe each example.**

1. the sound of many birds singing on a spring morning _____

2. the two halves of a human face _____

3. a sudden change from rain to bright sunshine _____

4. keep yourself from spending money on silly purchases _____

5. change from a formal lunch into a food fight _____

## EXERCISE D  More Prefix Samples

**Use a dictionary to find four additional words that begin with the prefixes introduced in this lesson. Write the words on the lines below. Check the word history, given in brackets in the dictionary entry, to confirm that the word begins with a prefix.**

1. _____

2. _____

3. _____

4. _____

# *Vocabulary Power*

## Lesson 28  Using Reading Skills
### Using a Dictionary: Multiple-Meaning Words

Many words have more than one meaning. In a dictionary entry, these meanings are listed by number from the most to the least common, or from general to specific, as in the entry below.

> **instrument** (in' strə ment) *n.* **1.** A means by which something is accomplished  **2.** A person who is used by another as a means or aid; a dupe  **3.** An implement that assists work; a tool, especially a small precision tool  **4.** A device for recording, measuring, or controlling  **5.** A device for producing music  **6.** A legal document

### EXERCISE A

**The word *instrument* appears in each sentence below. Write the number of the specific definition that fits the meaning of the word as it is used in the sentence.**

_____ 1. By delivering the message, the ship's cabin boy became an **instrument** of death.

_____ 2. The world-famous violinist always buys a separate seat on the airplane for his **instrument**.

_____ 3. The hygienist uses a sharp **instrument** to scrape the plaque carefully from your teeth.

_____ 4. The **instrument** that states what will happen to a person's possessions after death is called a will.

_____ 5. Weather forecasters use an **instrument** called a barometer to measure atmospheric pressure.

_____ 6. The Internet is the **instrument** whereby Jake and Nat became friends.

### EXERCISE B

**Answer each question using the information in the dictionary entry above.**

1. What is a synonym for a person who is an instrument?

_____

2. What is a synonym for an instrument that is used to do some kind of work?

_____

3. Why is the meaning "a legal document" listed last in the entry?

_____

4. Is it more appropriate to refer to a surgeon's tools or a carpenter's tools as instruments?

_____

5. What is the most general meaning of *instrument*?

_____

*Vocabulary Power*

## Review: Unit 6

**EXERCISE**

**Circle the word that best completes each sentence.**

1. Mike's blunt way of speaking is (unsightly, offensive, raucous) to many people.

2. Some chess players (hinder, maneuver, conceive) their pieces to bring the queen into play early in the game.

3. Now that the library has a new addition, there is (ample, adjacent, uniform) room for the books.

4. If the disagreement between the two countries is not resolved, violence could (simultaneously, eventually, moderately) result.

5. Carmen will try to (intercept, restrain, foster) Doug on his way to school to give him the news.

6. The (remote, uniform, abrupt) cabin is located deep in the wilderness, far from any town or village.

7. A new concrete dam will (abstain, squander, restrain) the water in the lake, but large gates in the dam will release water into the stream below from time to time.

8. Olivia was (shrewd, prudent, audacious) in figuring out that the cause of the mysterious damage was a baby raccoon.

9. The police detective used the crime scene clues to (degenerate, deduce, restrain) who had committed the crime.

10. The sample of river water Alan tested proved to be (obstinate, remote, toxic).

# Vocabulary Power

## Test: Unit 6

**PART A**

**Circle the letter of the answer that best completes each sentence.**

1. You would be most likely to jest with _____.
   a. a stranger    b. a good friend    c. a teacher    d. a salesperson

2. An obstinate person might say, _____
   a. "You'll never change my mind."    c. "You look wonderful today."
   b. "You'd better get out of my way."    d. "You and I should cooperate."

3. An example of an unsightly place is _____.
   a. a tiny town with only one stoplight    c. a park covered with trash
   b. a beautiful mountain    d. a dark cave

4. A moderately sunny place would be _____.
   a. often but not always sunny    c. sunny all the time
   b. never sunny    d. sunny once a month

5. If the trees in a woods are uniform, they are _____.
   a. not healthy    c. joined together at the roots
   b. all the same size and shape    d. without leaves

6. If two stores are adjacent, they are _____.
   a. across the street from each other    c. next to each other
   b. on top of each other    d. far apart from each other

7. A tactful hostess would _____.
   a. change the subject when two guests begin to argue
   b. offer everyone second helpings of dessert
   c. plan ahead to make sure there was enough food
   d. welcome each person at the door

8. A disagreement could degenerate into a(n) _____.
   a. agreement    b. fight    c. debate    d. song

9. If you were a competent soccer player, you would probably _____.
   a. make the team    c. be cut from the team
   b. be the best player on the team    d. be admired for your unusual style

# Vocabulary Power *continued*

10. A person who wants to lose weight might abstain from _____.
    a. exercise
    c. wearing loose clothing
    b. eating desserts
    d. eating fruits and vegetables

## PART B

**Circle the word that best completes each sentence.**

1. His (prudent, competent, abrupt) manner did not win any friends at his monthly lodge meetings.

2. The (uniform, symphony, remote) presented a wonderful piece by Tchaikovsky last month.

3. Many insects will continue to (degenerate, thrive, maneuver) in even the harshest conditions.

4. Anita was (dejected, prosperous, remote) after her job prospects fell through.

5. Larry got the office (offensive, symmetrical, adjacent) to the stairwell.

## PART C

**Circle the letter of the word that means most nearly the *opposite* of the boldfaced word.**

1. **foster**
    a. discourage       b. promote       c. fake       d. free

2. **hinder**
    a. imagine       b. waste       c. help       d. block

3. **concise**
    a. brief       b. wordy       c. sharp       d. pleasant

4. **precise**
    a. proper       b. incorrect       c. exact       d. unattractive

5. **prevail**
    a. overcome       b. fail       c. prevent       d. conceive

# Vocabulary Power

## Lesson 29  Word Choices

A single event can often cause you to go through a wide range of emotions and actions. The words in this list can help you describe these different dimensions of your experience.

**Word List**

| | | | |
|---|---|---|---|
| brood | flounder | resourceful | sufficient |
| efficient | potent | saturate | uncanny |
| enticing | rash | | |

**EXERCISE A**  Synonyms

**Each boldfaced word below is paired with a synonym whose meaning you probably know. Think of other words related to the synonym and write them on the line provided. Then, look up the vocabulary word in a dictionary and write its meaning.**

1. **brood** : worry _____

   Dictionary definition _____

2. **resourceful** : inventive _____

   Dictionary definition _____

3. **potent** : powerful _____

   Dictionary definition _____

4. **enticing** : tempting _____

   Dictionary definition _____

5. **rash** : reckless _____

   Dictionary definition _____

6. **uncanny** : eerie _____

   Dictionary definition _____

7. **sufficient** : enough _____

   Dictionary definition _____

8. **flounder** : blunder _____

   Dictionary definition _____

9. **saturate** : soak _____

Dictionary definition _____

10. **efficient** : effective _____

Dictionary definition _____

### EXERCISE B   Vocabulary Choices
**Circle the word that best completes each sentence.**

1. Mom's blue pitcher holds (efficient, sufficient, resourceful) milk to fill four large glasses.

2. Randall soon regretted his (rash, uncanny, enticing) decision.

3. We need a heavy rain to (flounder, brood, saturate) the ground and help the corn grow.

4. The (sufficient, uncanny, resourceful) camper piled up pine needles to make a bed.

### EXERCISE C   Word Meanings
**Write the word that best fits each example.**

1. a furnace that produces much heat using little fuel          _____

2. a dish of cookies that makes you want to take one          _____

3. a psychic's ability to predict the future          _____

4. think gloomily and at length about not being popular          _____

5. stumble clumsily through knee-deep mud          _____

6. a strong medicine that provides relief from many aches and pains          _____

### EXERCISE D   Multiple-Meaning Words
**Look up the boldfaced words in a dictionary. On a separate sheet of paper, write the
dictionary definition of each word as it is used in the sentence.**

1. After Grandpa and I went fishing, we fried the **flounder** we caught.

2. The climber started up the mountain, then began to **flounder**.

3. When Joel ate too many eggs, he broke out in a **rash**.

4. In April, there was a **rash** of bank robberies.

5. The robin hovered near her **brood**.

6. She began to **brood** about the exam.

## *Vocabulary Power*

## Lesson 30  Suffixes That Form Verbs

A suffix is a syllable placed after a word root to change or add to its meaning or to change the word's part of speech. The suffix *-ize* means "to become like" or "to treat with," *-ate* means "to cause to become," and *-fy* means "to make." For example, the word *finalize* (*final + ize*) means "to become final," and *activate* (*active + ate*) means "to become active." Words ending in *-ize, -ate,* and *-fy* are always verbs.

| Word List | | | |
| --- | --- | --- | --- |
| clarify | mobilize | ruminate | vacillate |
| implicate | modify | tyrannize | verify |
| itemize | revitalize | | |

### EXERCISE A  Synonyms

**Each boldfaced word below is paired with a synonym whose meaning you probably know. Underline the verb suffix in the boldfaced word. Then, look up the word in a dictionary and write its meaning.**

1. **clarify** : explain _____

2. **tyrannize** : oppress _____

3. **mobilize** : activate _____

4. **modify** : alter _____

5. **implicate** : mix up _____

6. **itemize** : list _____

7. **vacillate** : waver _____

8. **revitalize** : renew _____

9. **verify** : prove _____

10. **ruminate** : reflect on _____

### EXERCISE B  Word Substitutions

**If the boldfaced word is used correctly in the sentence, write *correct* above it. If not, draw a line through it and write the correct vocabulary word above it.**

1. Marguerite began to **revitalize** all the things she wanted to take on her trip to the beach.

2. Don't try to **implicate** that this mess is my fault!

3. We want to **mobilize** the entire student body for the cleanup project.

## ♭ *Vocabulary Power* continued

4. Before I make up my mind what to do, I need more time to **tyrannize**.

5. We used an almanac to **clarify** that Ankara is the capital of Turkey.

6. Her opinion seems to **implicate** from one extreme to the other constantly.

7. Without laws and law enforcement, criminals could **tyrannize** the public freely.

8. Molly wanted to **modify** her position so there could be no misunderstandings.

9. Why did you attempt to **modify** the agreement without my permission?

10. The city council set aside funds to **itemize** the waterfront section of town.

### EXERCISE C  Word Meanings
**Write the word that best fits each example.**

1. say yes to something, then no, then yes _____

2. use a diagram to make a process easier to understand _____

3. add a wheelchair ramp to the entrance of a building _____

4. rule a country by using power in a cruel way _____

5. make a downtown area lively and productive again _____

6. pondering which college to attend _____

7. to imply that Jimmy broke your toy car _____

8. a family leaving to visit relatives _____

9. asking questions to be sure the truth was told _____

10. a list of groceries for Thanksgiving dinner _____

### EXERCISE D  Explanation Paragraph
**Have you ever seen a cow *ruminate*? Look up the words *rumen, ruminant,* and *ruminate* and read their definitions. On a separate sheet of paper, write a short paragraph explaining how human beings are similar to ruminants when they ruminate.**

*Vocabulary Power*

## Lesson 31  Compound Words

Some words are a combination of two or more other words. *Snowstorm, pocket-size,* and *plus sign* are all compound words. A compound word may be spelled as one word, with a hyphen, or with a space between the combined words.

**Word List**

| | | | |
|---|---|---|---|
| backtrack | heat lightning | spot-check | sugarcoat |
| good-humored | self-concept | straightforward | topsy-turvy |
| headroom | shortchange | | |

**EXERCISE A  Matching Definitions**

**Analyze the words in each compound word to match the compound with the correct definition.**

_____ 1. to go back over the way by which you have come

_____ 2. direct in manner or expression

_____ 3. cheerful; good-natured

_____ 4. vivid flashes of light without thunder on a hot day

_____ 5. image that a person has of himself or herself

_____ 6. to give someone less than what is due to him or her

_____ 7. to check or inspect something in an irregular way

_____ 8. upside-down; in a state of disorder or confusion

_____ 9. to make superficially attractive

_____10. space above one's head for standing, sitting, or moving

**EXERCISE B  Word Clues**

**Write the word that best fits the clue.**

1. a person who is always pleasant and cooperative    _____

2. a coach's attempt to cushion team "cuts"    _____

3. the space in a car between your head and the ceiling    _____

4. late-night electrical storm without rain    _____

5. idea of yourself as a responsible person    _____

## Vocabulary Power *continued*

**6.** to retrace your steps to find something you dropped _____

**7.** to inspect new products every now and then at a factory _____

**8.** person who tells the truth without sugarcoating it _____

**9.** to give someone eight tickets when you promised ten _____

**10.** messy room where young children have played all day _____

### EXERCISE C  Word Meanings
**Answer each question.**

**1.** What is your **self-concept?**

_____

**2.** What is something that a store owner might **spot-check?**

_____

_____

**3.** Describe a situation when a person might **sugarcoat** the truth.

_____

**4.** Where and when would you expect to find **heat lightning?**

_____

**5.** In what situation might a person need to **backtrack?**

_____

**6.** Give an example of **shortchange** that involves money.

_____

**7.** What might a **good-humored** person say to you?

_____

**8.** What is a place where the **headroom** might be limited?

_____

**9.** What could turn your life **topsy-turvy?**

_____

**10.** Give an example of **straightforward** instructions.

_____

# Vocabulary Power

## Lesson 32 Using Reading Skills
### Learning from Context: Comparison/Contrast

When you encounter a new word in your reading, you can often use clues from the material in which it appears, called the context, to figure out its meaning. Sometimes, the new word is compared to or contrasted with more familiar words that have similar or opposite meanings. Certain words, such as *like, also,* and *too,* may signal a comparison. Other words, such as *but, unlike,* and *however,* may signal a contrast.

**Comparison**
**Kelly is a beginner; Jan is *also* a novice.**
Explanation: The word *also* signals a comparison: Kelly and Jan are alike. So you can guess that *novice* may mean "beginner."

**Contrast**
**Feral dogs, *unlike* tame dogs, roam in packs and attack smaller animals.**
Explanation: The word *unlike* signals a contrast: feral dogs and tame dogs are not alike. So you can guess that *feral* may mean "untame" or "wild."

### EXERCISE A

**In each sentence, circle the word that signals a comparison or contrast. Then, write the boldfaced word and its probable meaning based on the context clues.**

1. In the story, Zadar is a **malevolent** character, unlike Sirena, who stands for goodness.

_____

2. The **cuisine** of Vietnam is similar to the food of Thailand.

_____

3. In contrast to other runners who dropped out of the race, Gwen showed **perseverance** until the end.

_____

4. My great-grandfather is an **octogenarian;** my great-aunt is also in her eighties.

_____

5. Roger found the beans quite **palatable,** but Nikki thought they tasted unpleasant.

_____

6. Clem has an **introverted** personality; however, his sister Tina is more outgoing.

_____

### EXERCISE B

**Choose two boldfaced words from Exercise A and check their meanings in a dictionary. Then, on a separate sheet of paper, write a sentence using each word.**

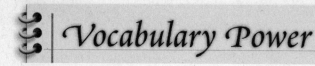

# Vocabulary Power

## Review: Unit 7

**Circle the word that best fits each example.**

1. decision made too quickly
   a. rash        b. good-humored        c. uncanny        d. straightforward

2. supernatural event in a movie
   a. efficient        b. topsy-turvy        c. uncanny        d. potent

3. lawn-care product that kills multiple kinds of weeds
   a. saturate        b. topsy-turvy        c. potent        d. resourceful

4. to explain a difficult grammatical concept
   a. verify        b. clarify        c. ruminate        d. shortchange

5. training that gives you an adequate understanding of rock climbing
   a. sufficient        b. potent        c. brood        d. good-humored

6. getting rid of old tires by grinding them up and using them as a ground cover in playgrounds
   a. brood        b. potent        c. rash        d. resourceful

7. a half-price trip to Hawaii
   a. topsy-turvy        b. rash        c. enticing        d. uncanny

8. a team of students washing a car in five minutes
   a. efficient        b. straightforward        c. good-humored        d. potent

9. laughing when you get hit in the face with a pie
   a. straightforward        b. rash        c. efficient        d. good-humored

10. to change a car by removing its fenders and replacing its tires
    a. itemize        b. modify        c. clarify        d. spot-check

**EXERCISE B**

**Circle the word that best completes each sentence.**

1. Could you give me an example to (modify, clarify, shortchange) what you mean by "cultured"?

2. There's no more time to (vacillate, revitalize, saturate); you have to make up your mind!

3. You should (clarify, itemize, saturate) the cloth with wood stain before wiping the table.

# Vocabulary Power

## Test: Unit 7

PART A

**Circle the letter of the correct definition for each word.**

1. rash
   - **a.** spoken harshly
   - **b.** done without careful thought
   - **c.** achieved with much effort
   - **d.** turned over in the mind slowly

2. flounder
   - **a.** examine closely
   - **b.** swim gracefully
   - **c.** bob up and down
   - **d.** struggle awkwardly

3. sufficient
   - **a.** dependable
   - **b.** enough
   - **c.** slight
   - **d.** powerful

4. clarify
   - **a.** make easier to understand
   - **b.** change in form or character
   - **c.** establish the truth
   - **d.** fill with fear

5. good-humored
   - **a.** clever
   - **b.** brave
   - **c.** cheerful
   - **d.** uncanny

6. tyrannize
   - **a.** attract
   - **b.** rule in a cruel manner
   - **c.** change one's mind often
   - **d.** ponder

7. itemize
   - **a.** shrink
   - **b.** buy
   - **c.** list
   - **d.** cancel

8. ruminate
   - **a.** soak in
   - **b.** check regularly
   - **c.** make a hasty decision
   - **d.** go over in the mind slowly

9. topsy-turvy
   - **a.** in a state of order
   - **b.** in a state of readiness
   - **c.** in a state of confusion
   - **d.** in a state of calm

10. **straightforward**
   a. insincere
   b. narrow
   c. direct
   d. fast

## PART B

**Circle the letter of the expression that best completes each sentence.**

1. If you **shortchange** someone, you treat the person _____.
   a. fairly
   b. unfairly
   c. pleasantly
   d. politely

2. A **self-concept** refers to _____.
   a. how friends think of you
   b. how you think of yourself
   c. how a psychologist might think of you
   d. how your family thinks of you

3. You could **modify** a bicycle by _____.
   a. replacing the handlebars with a different style
   b. washing it
   c. trading it for another model
   d. riding it fast

4. To **verify** something is to find out if it is _____.
   a. different
   b. fair
   c. true
   d. new

5. Something that could **revitalize** a tired person on a hot day is _____.
   a. having a cool, refreshing drink
   b. getting a new car
   c. doing outdoor chores
   d. riding on a crowded train

# Vocabulary Power

## Lesson 33  Using Synonyms

Planting a garden, raising a pet, walking in the woods, or strolling at the seashore can all make you feel a connection to nature. You can use the words in this lesson to describe that connection to nature.

**Word List**

| | | | |
|---|---|---|---|
| cower | fiction | lunge | scurry |
| drastic | glee | regal | sluggish |
| extension | hostile | | |

### EXERCISE A  Synonyms

**Each boldfaced word is paired with a synonym whose meaning you probably know. Think of other related words or ideas and write them on the line provided. Then, look up the word in a dictionary and write its meaning.**

1. **sluggish** : inactive _____

   Dictionary definition _____

2. **drastic** : extreme _____

   Dictionary definition _____

3. **glee** : happiness _____

   Dictionary definition _____

4. **scurry** : scamper _____

   Dictionary definition _____

5. **fiction** : something made up _____

   Dictionary definition _____

6. **cower** : pull away in fear _____

   Dictionary definition _____

7. **hostile** : unfriendly _____

   Dictionary definition _____

8. **extension** : a lengthening _____

   Dictionary definition _____

## Vocabulary Power *continued*

9. **regal** : royal _____

Dictionary definition _____

10. **lunge** : move suddenly _____

Dictionary definition _____

### EXERCISE B  Word Meanings
**Write the vocabulary word that best completes each sentence.**

1. The general studied the _____ army through his binoculars.

2. I gasped as I watched the snake suddenly _____ for the mouse.

3. The beautiful horse shook its _____ mane as if it were a king.

4. Mr. Green built a one-hundred-foot _____ to his fence.

5. The lottery winner squealed with _____ when her name was announced.

6. Snowball, our new kitten, will _____ fearfully under the bed whenever a guest arrives.

7. We watched the squirrel grasp a chestnut and quickly _____ up the tree.

8. Darla's ridiculous story about meeting Tom Cruise is just _____.

9. Jacob's solution to the problem was far too _____, so we decided on a less extreme plan.

10. Everyone felt _____ after eating the huge Thanksgiving dinner!

### EXERCISE C  Multiple-Meaning Words
**Many words have more than one meaning. Look up the boldfaced words in a dictionary. Write the definition that best fits each word.**

1. Yelling at Susan was a **hostile** act.

   _____

2. The desert is a **hostile** environment for many creatures.

   _____

3. In the operating room, the scalpel is an **extension** of the doctor's hand.

   _____

4. Felicity was given an **extension** on her research paper.

   _____

# *Vocabulary Power*

## Lesson 34  Homophones and Homographs

Homophones are words that have the same pronunciation but different spellings and meanings. The words *there, their,* and *they're* are homophones. They are pronounced the same, but each word has a different meaning and spelling. Homographs are words that are spelled the same but have different pronunciations and meanings. Some common homographs are *wind* (moving air) and *wind* (to twist or roll up), *tear* (to rip) and *tear* (moisture from the eyes). Other homographs have the same spelling *and* pronunciation, but different meanings. *Fair* (a farming show and exhibition) and *fair* (average, not good or bad) are examples of this kind of homograph.

| Word List | | | |
|---|---|---|---|
| air | heir | principal | vice |
| altar | idle | principle | vise |
| alter | idol | | |

### EXERCISE A  Dictionary Definitions

**Look up each word in a dictionary and write its definition. Then, write a sentence of your own.**

1. alter _____

_____

2. altar _____

_____

3. vice _____

_____

4. vise _____

_____

5. principal _____

_____

6. principle _____

_____

7. air _____

_____

8. heir _____

_____

# Vocabulary Power *continued*

9. idle _____

_____

10. idol _____

_____

## EXERCISE B  Usage
**Write the vocabulary word that best completes the sentence.**

1. The police captain promised to stamp out _____ in the inner city.

2. One important _____ in American law is that all people are considered innocent until they are proven guilty.

3. When his _____, John Elway, retired, Andy lost interest in football.

4. The priest bowed before the _____ and began to pray.

5. The _____ of our school received an award for his antilittering program.

6. Because John was his aunt's only living relative, he became _____ to $100,000.

7. It is too late to _____ the school play–we will just have to find another actor.

8. Before he sawed the board in half, Rex placed it in a(n) _____.

9. Every spring Grandma felt it was necessary to _____ all the carpets in the house.

10. Those kids standing _____ around the video arcade should find something helpful to do.

# *Vocabulary Power*

## Lesson 35  Borrowed Words

English contains many words borrowed from other languages. Some borrowed words look just like English, but others look unusual or different from most English words. Dictionaries usually give a borrowed word's history and its meaning in the original language if the original meaning differs from the English meaning. In this lesson, you'll learn some common borrowed words.

**Word List**

| banjo | enthusiasm | opossum | stoop |
| bungalow | gourmet | rendezvous | thug |
| camouflage | lariat | | |

**EXERCISE A**  **Dictionary Definitions**

**Look up each boldfaced word in a dictionary. Write its meaning in English. Then, give the information about its history and its meaning in the original language.**

1. rendezvous _____

    From _____ Original meaning _____

2. camouflage _____

    From _____ Original meaning _____

3. gourmet _____

    From _____ Original meaning _____

4. enthusiasm _____

    From _____ Original meaning _____

5. lariat _____

    From _____ Original meaning _____

6. bungalow _____

    From _____ Original meaning _____

7. thug _____

    From _____ Original meaning _____

8. banjo _____

    From _____ Original meaning _____

# Vocabulary Power *continued*

9. stoop _____

   From _____ Original meaning _____

10. opossum _____

    From _____ Original meaning _____

## EXERCISE B  Word Meanings
**Write the vocabulary word that best completes each sentence.**

1. The detective watched the dangerous-looking _____ standing in the shadows.

2. With a snap of his wrist, the cowboy tossed the _____ around the calf's neck.

3. Let's set up a(n) _____ at the coffee shop after the movie.

4. Alana approached her new job as manager of the clothing store with great _____.

5. The newly married couple moved into the small _____ near the beach.

## EXERCISE C  Writing Summaries
**Here are the titles of two new movies. Use your imagination and at least one vocabulary word from this lesson to write a short plot summary of each movie.**

1. *My Dinner with Seymour*

   _____

   _____

   _____

   _____

   _____

2. *Threatmaster, Part 2: This Time It's Personal*

   _____

   _____

   _____

   _____

   _____

# Vocabulary Power

## Lesson 36  Using Test-Taking Skills
### Analogies

Analogies show the relationship of one thing to another thing. For example, when you say that you love apple pie as much as your sister loves chocolate cake, you are making an analogy. Your relationship to apple pie is the same as your sister's relationship to chocolate cake; they're your favorite desserts. Analogies are sometimes expressed in this way:

you : apple pie :: your sister : chocolate cake

Notice that *you* and *your sister* are in the same position in each pair as *apple pie* and *chocolate cake*. Many kinds of relationships can be expressed by analogies. Some of the most common are *antonyms,* or opposites, and *synonyms,* or words that mean the same thing. Others are *differences of degree* (warm : roasting :: cool : freezing), *one of a kind* (oak : tree :: bass : fish), *cause and effect* (sadness: crying :: happiness : smiling), *parts of a whole* (player : team :: musician : orchestra), *location* (scorpion : desert :: dolphin : ocean), and *person related to skill, tool, or other element* (carpenter : hammer :: math teacher : calculator). The first step in understanding an analogy is to analyze the relationship. Then, look for the choice that best matches the analogy.

### EXERCISE

**Circle the letter of the choice that best completes the analogy. Then, write the type of analogy that is being expressed.**

1. chapter : novel :: _____

   **a.** artist : painting

   **b.** lyrics : song

   **c.** article : newspaper

   **d.** page : leaf

   Type of analogy: _____

2. volleyball player : gymnasium :: _____

   **a.** student : classroom

   **b.** sock : shoe

   **c.** announcer : microphone

   **d.** police : criminal

   Type of analogy: _____

3. idle : busy :: _____

   **a.** clever : dull

   **b.** rapid : swift

   **c.** interested : skillful

   **d.** happy : frown

   Type of analogy: _____

4. judge : wisdom :: _____

   **a.** teacher : homework

   **b.** police officer : public safety

   **c.** carpenter : nails

   **d.** editor : pens

   Type of analogy: _____

# Vocabulary Power

## Review: Unit 8

**EXERCISE**

**Circle the word in parentheses that best completes each sentence.**

1. The thief's capture was greeted with (camouflage, glee, fiction) in the village.

2. The (drastic, principal, hostile) reason I am opposed to the program is that it requires students to stay out too late.

3. The Rams' cheerleaders increased the fans' (extension, rendezvous, enthusiasm) by having them do the wave.

4. The roof is so high that we will need to put a(n) (altar, lariat, extension) on the ladder.

5. Midori is my brother's (heir, idol, principal) because she plays the violin with such emotion and skill.

6. The troops received a(n) (regal, idle, hostile) reaction from the people of the town they attacked.

7. When my dad shakes my hand, my fingers feel as though they are being squeezed in a(n) (lariat, vise, altar).

8. Although the tales about Robin Hood sound true, many of them are (vice, fiction, principal).

9. Even though I slept twelve hours, I still feel (hostile, sluggish, regal).

10. Your plane ticket does not permit you to (cower, air, alter) your trip plan in any way.

11. The lion crouched behind a tree, ready to (cower, lunge, scurry) at the zebra.

12. Let's arrange a(n) (rendezvous, vice, extension) with the Italian students to talk about their culture.

13. Matthew's gerbils become fearful and (lunge, cower, alter) whenever anyone looks at them.

14. According to the will, the dead man's only (camouflage, principal, heir) is his long-lost nephew.

15. The Golden Rule is a very good (fiction, principle, vice) by which to live.

# Vocabulary Power

## Test: Unit 8

### PART A

**Circle the letter of the word that best completes each sentence.**

1. Deanna looked so _____ in her costume that she could have been a real queen.
   a. idle            b. drastic          c. regal            d. hostile

2. Everyone watched the _____, where the priest was performing the royal wedding.
   a. altar           b. alter            c. lariat           d. bungalow

3. Lift that old log and some unusual insects will probably _____ out.
   a. cower           b. air              c. alter            d. scurry

4. The spies wore _____ outfits so they wouldn't be seen by the enemy.
   a. camouflage      b. drastic          c. hostile          d. regal

5. Mama came out on the front _____ to see what all the noise was about.
   a. altar           b. vise             c. bungalow         d. stoop

6. The mayor promised to stamp out _____ in the city, no matter how widespread.
   a. fiction         b. vice             c. enthusiasm       d. glee

7. The villain tried to _____ at the sheriff and grab his pistol.
   a. scurry          b. cower            c. lunge            d. alter

8. Telling the truth is one _____ that I consider important.
   a. principle       b. principal        c. enthusiasm       d. vice

9. For dinner, the _____ chef prepared snails in cream sauce.
   a. idle            b. gourmet          c. sluggish         d. hostile

10. No _____ to Michael Jordan's title as the world's best basketball player has yet appeared.
    a. heir           b. idol             c. air              d. principal

### PART B

**Circle the letter of the word that is an *antonym*, or the opposite of, the boldfaced word or words.**

1. **friendly**
   a. hostile         b. sluggish         c. drastic          d. regal

2. **keep secret**
   a. cower           b. scurry           c. lunge            d. air

# *Vocabulary Power* continued

3. common
   a. sluggish      b. hostile      c. regal      d. idle

4. full of energy
   a. drastic      b. sluggish      c. regal      d. hostile

5. least important
   a. drastic      b. idle      c. principal      d. sluggish

6. lack of interest
   a. enthusiasm      b. extension      c. principal      d. camouflage

7. sadness
   a. vice      b. extension      c. rendezvous      d. glee

8. busy
   a. idle      b. hostile      c. regal      d. principal

9. keep the same
   a. cower      b. alter      c. lunge      d. air

10. truth
    a. fiction      b. extension      c. enthusiasm      d. lariat

abrupt   ə brupt´

abstain   ab stān´

abstract   ab´strakt

academic   ak´ə dem´ik

acronym   ak´rə nim´

acutely   ə kūt´lē

adjacent   ə jā´sənt

administer   ad min´is tər

advantage   ad van´tij

advocate   ad´və kāt´

aggravate   ag´rə vāt´

agile   aj´əl

air   ār

align   ə līn´

altar   ôl´tər

alter   ôl´tər

amenable   ə mē´nə bəl

ample   am´pəl

anarchy   an´ər kē

annual   an´ū əl

anticipation   an tis´ə pā´shən

antidote   an´ti dōt´

apathy   ap´ə thē

appalling   ə pô´ling

arid   ar´id

assert   ə surt´

assess   ə ses´

asset   as´et

audacious   ô dā´shəs

auditorium   ô´də tôr´ē əm

auditory   ô´də tôr´ē

aviator   ā´vē ā´tər

backtrack   bak´trak´

banjo   ban´jō

barren   bar´ən

behemoth   bi hē´məth

beneficial   ben´ə fish´əl

bewildered   bi wil´dərd

bias   bī´əs

brink   bringk

brood   brōōd

bungalow   bung´gə lō´

burden   burd´ən

camouflage   kam´ə fläzh´

catastrophe   kə tas´trə fē´

chronic   kron´ik

chronicle   kron´i kəl

circumstance   sur´kəm stans´

civic   siv´ik

clarify   klar´ə fī´

collaborate   kə lab´ə rāt´

communism   kom´yə niz´əm

compassion   kəm pash´ən

compensation   kom´pən sā´shən

competent   kom´pət ənt

comply   kəm plī´

comprehend   kom´pri hend´

conceive   kən sēv´

concise   kən sīs´

condemnation   kon´dem nā´shən

confront   kən frunt´

consent   kən sent´

consolation   kon sə lā´shən

conviction   kən vik´shən

cower   kou´ər

crucial   krōō´shəl

cuisine   kwi zēn´

deduce   di dōōs´

defiant   di fī´ənt

degenerate   di jen´ə rāt´

dejected   di jek´tid

delectable   di lek´tə bəl

deport   di pôrt´

desolate   des´ə lit

despicable   des´pi kə bəl

detach   di tach´

devise   di vīz´

dictate   dik´tāt

dictator   dik´tā´tər

diction   dik´shən

dignity   dig´nə tē

disoriented   dis ôr´i ent´id

dispense   dis pens´

displace   dis plās´

dissension   di sen´shən

dissent   di sent´

distinctive   dis tingk´tiv

divulge   di vulj´

docile   dos´əl

documentation   dok´yə men tā´shən

drab   drab

drastic   dras´tik

drastically   dras´tik lē

dwindle   dwind´əl

dynamic   dī nam´ik

dynasty   dī´nəs tē

eerie   ēr´ē

efficient   i fish´ənt

emerge   i murj´

enthusiasm   en thōō´zē az´əm

enticing   en tīs´ing

erratic   ə rat´ik

eventually   i ven´chōō ə lē

exhibit   ig zib´it

exotic   ig zot´ik

extension   iks ten´shən

exuberant   ig zōō´bər ənt

falter   fôl´tər

fiction   fik´shən

flounder   floun´dər

foster   fôs´tər

frail   frāl

frenzy   fren´zē

gauge   gāj

glee   glē

good-humored   good´hū´mərd

gourmet   goor mā´

grave   grāv

hardy   här´dē

headroom   hed´rōōm

heat lightning   hēt´līt´ning

heir   ār

hinder   hin´dər

hostile   host´əl

hydrant   hī´drənt

hydroelectric   hī´drō i lek´trik

idle   īd´əl

idol   īd´əl

illegible   i lej´ə bəl

illuminate   i lōō´mə nāt´

illumination   i lōō´mə nā´shən

imbibe   im bīb´

improvise   im´prə vīz´

inaudible   in ô´də bəl

incompetent   in kom´pət ənt

indifferent   in dif´ər ənt

inquisitive   in kwiz´ə tiv

inscription   in skrip´shən

instrument   in´strə mənt

intercept   in´tər sept´

intimidated   in tim´ə dāt´id

introverted   in´trə vurt´id

invert   in vurt´

investor   in vest´ər

irrational   i rash´ən əl

itemize   ī´tə mīz´

jest   jest

lariat   lar´ē ət

lethal   lē´thəl

lofty   lôf´tē

loom   lōōm

lunge   lunj

malevolent   mə lev´ə lənt

malfunction   mal´fungk´shən

maneuver   mə nōō´vər

manufacture   man´yə fak´chər

maverick   mav´ər ik

mobility   mō bil´ə tē

mobilize   mō´bə līz´

mock   mok

moderately   mod´ər it lē

modest   mod´ist

modify   mod´ə fī´

momentary   mō´mən ter´ē

monarch   mon´ərk

motive   mō´tiv

murky   mur´kē

naive   nä ēv´

neglected   ni glekt´id

nimble   nim´bəl

nonsense   non´sens

nurture   nur´chər

obscure   əb skyoor´

obsessed   əb sest´

obstinate   ob´stə nit

octogenarian   ok´tə jə nār´ē ən

offensive   ə fen´siv

ominous   om´ə nəs

opossum   ə pos´əm

opportunity   op´ər tōō´nə tē

oppose ə pōz´

optimist op´tə mist

ordeal ôr dēl´

outpost out´pōst´

palatable pal´ə tə bəl

passive pas´iv

paternal pə turn´əl

patriotic pā´trē ot´ik

perilous per´ə ləs

perplexity pər plek´sə tē

perseverance pur´sə vēr´əns

pinnacle pin´ə kəl

pitfall pit´fôl´

portable pôr´tə bəl

portly pôrt´lē

posterity pos ter´ə tē

postscript pōst´skript´

postseason pōst´sē´zən

potent pōt´ənt

prank prangk

preamble prē´am´bəl

precise pri sīs´

preconceived prē´kən sēvd´

predate prē dāt´

predetermine prē´di tur´min

premature prē´mə choor´

premonition prē´mə nish´ən

prerequisite prē rek´wə zit

prescribe pri skrīb´

presume pri zōōm´

prevail pri vāl´

preview prē´vū

primary prī´mer´ē

principal prin´sə pəl

principle prin´sə pəl

propel prə pel´

prosperous pros´pər əs

provide prə vīd´

providence prov´ə dəns

prudent prōōd´ənt

pursue pər sōō´

rash rash

rashly rash´lē

raucous rô´kəs

ravenous rav´ə nəs

realism rē´ə liz´əm

refuge ref´ūj

regal rē´gəl

relinquish ri ling´kwish

remote ri mōt´

rendezvous rän´də vōō´

renegade ren´ə gād´

resent ri zent´

resigned ri zīnd´

resilient ri zil´yənt

resourceful ri sôrs´fəl

restore ri stôr´

restrain ri strān´

revitalize ri vī´təl īz

revoke ri vōk´

ruminate rōō´mə nāt´

sanctuary sangk´chōō er´ē

saturate sach´ə rāt´

scour skour

scribble skrib´əl

scurry skur´ē

self-concept self´kon´sept

sensitize sen´sə tīz´

sentimental sen´tə ment´əl

shortchange shôrt´chānj´

shrewd shrōōd

shun shun

simultaneously sī´məl tā´nē əs lē

sluggish slug´ish

soberly sō´bər lē

somberly som´bər lē

specify spes´ə fī´

speculate spek´yə lāt´

speculation spek´yə lā´shən

spoilage spoi´lij

spontaneous spon tā´nē əs

spot-check spot´chek´

squander skwon´dər

status stā´təs

stoop stōōp

straightforward strāt´fôr´wərd

sufficient sə fish´ənt

sugarcoat shoog´ər kōt´

surge surj

symbol sim´bəl

symmetrical   si met′ri kəl
sympathy   sim′pə thē
symphony   sim′fə nē
synchronize   sing′krə nīz′
tactful   takt′fəl
tantalize   tant′əl īz′
temptation   temp tā′shən
termination   tur′mə nā′shən
thrive   thrīv
throng   thrông
thug   thug
topical   top′i kəl
topsy-turvy   top′sē tur′vē
toxic   tok′sik
tranquil   trang′kwəl
traumatic   trô mat′ik
tripod   trī′pod′
trivial   triv′ē əl
tyrannize   tir′ə nīz′
unabridged   un′ə brijd′

uncanny   un kan′ē
undermine   un′dər mīn′
uniform   u¯′nə fôrm′
unscathed   un skāthd′
unsightly   un sīt′lē
vacillate   vas′ə lāt′
vary   vār′ē
vendor   ven′dər
verify   ver′ə fī′
versatile   vur′sə til
version   vur′zhən
vice   vīs
vigor   vig′ər
vise   vīs
visible   viz′ə bəl
vital   vīt′əl
wholeheartedly   hōl′här′tid lē
wily   wī′lē
zest   zest